COMPUTER SCIENCE, TECHNOLOGY AND APPLICATIONS

MALWARE AND COMPUTER SECURITY INCIDENTS

HANDLING GUIDES

COMPUTER SCIENCE, TECHNOLOGY AND APPLICATIONS

Additional books in this series can be found on Nova's website under the Series tab.

Additional E-books in this series can be found on Nova's website under the E-book tab.

COMPUTER SCIENCE, TECHNOLOGY AND APPLICATIONS

MALWARE AND COMPUTER SECURITY INCIDENTS

HANDLING GUIDES

MARK BORRELLI
EDITOR

nova publishers
New York

For permission to use material from this book please contact us:
Telephone 631-231-7269; Fax 631-231-8175
Web Site: http://www.novapublishers.com

Additional color graphics may be available in the e-book version of this book.

Library of Congress Cataloging-in-Publication Data

ISBN: 978-1-62948-191-3

Published by Nova Science Publishers, Inc. † New York

CONTENTS

PREFACE

Chapter 1 – Malware, also known as malicious code, refers to a program that is covertly inserted into another program with the intent to destroy data, run destructive or intrusive programs, or otherwise compromise the confidentiality, integrity, or availability of the victim's data, applications, or operating system. Malware is the most common external threat to most hosts, causing widespread damage and disruption and necessitating extensive recovery efforts within most organizations. This publication provides recommendations for improving an organization's malware incident prevention measures. It also gives extensive recommendations for enhancing an organization's existing incident response capability so that it is better prepared to handle malware incidents, particularly widespread ones.

Chapter 2 - Computer security incident response has become an important component of information technology (IT) programs. Because performing incident response effectively is a complex undertaking, establishing a successful incident response capability requires substantial planning and resources. This publication assists organizations in establishing computer security incident response capabilities and handling incidents efficiently and effectively. This publication provides guidelines for incident handling, particularly for analyzing incident-related data and determining the appropriate response to each incident. The guidelines can be followed independently of particular hardware platforms, operating systems, protocols, or applications.

In: Malware and Computer Security Incidents ISBN: 978-1-62948-191-3
Editor: Mark Borrelli

Chapter 1

GUIDE TO MALWARE INCIDENT PREVENTION AND HANDLING FOR DESKTOPS AND LAPTOPS*

Murugiah Souppaya and Karen Scarfone

SUMMARY

Malware, also known as malicious code, refers to a program that is covertly inserted into another program with the intent to destroy data, run destructive or intrusive programs, or otherwise compromise the confidentiality, integrity, or availability of the victim's data, applications, or operating system. Malware is the most common external threat to most hosts, causing widespread damage and disruption and necessitating extensive recovery efforts within most organizations. This publication provides recommendations for improving an organization's malware incident prevention measures. It also gives extensive recommendations for enhancing an organization's existing incident response capability so that it is better prepared to handle malware incidents, particularly widespread ones.

---

* This is an edited, reformatted and augmented version of NIST Special Publication 800-83; Revision 1 dated July 2013.

EXECUTIVE SUMMARY

Malware, also known as malicious code, refers to a program that is covertly inserted into another program with the intent to destroy data, run destructive or intrusive programs, or otherwise compromise the confidentiality, integrity, or availability of the victim's data, applications, or operating system. Malware is the most common external threat to most hosts, causing widespread damage and disruption and necessitating extensive recovery efforts within most organizations. Organizations also face similar threats from a few forms of non-malware threats that are often associated with malware. One of these forms that has become commonplace is phishing, which is using deceptive computer-based means to trick individuals into disclosing sensitive information.

This publication provides recommendations for improving an organization's malware incident prevention measures. It also gives extensive recommendations for enhancing an organization's existing incident response capability so that it is better prepared to handle malware incidents, particularly widespread ones. This revision of the publication, Revision 1, updates material throughout the publication to reflect the changes in threats and incidents. Unlike most malware threats several years ago, which tended to be fast-spreading and easy to notice, many of today's malware threats are more stealthy, specifically designed to quietly, slowly spread to other hosts, gathering information over extended periods of time and eventually leading to exfiltration of sensitive data and other negative impacts.

Implementing the following recommendations should facilitate more efficient and effective malware incident response activities for Federal departments and agencies.

Organizations Should Develop and Implement an Approach to Malware Incident Prevention

Organizations should plan and implement an approach to malware incident prevention based on the attack vectors that are most likely to be used currently and in the near future. Because the effectiveness of prevention techniques may vary depending on the environment (i.e., a technique that works well in a managed environment might be ineffective in a non-managed environment), organizations should choose preventive methods that are well-suited to their environment and hosts. An organization's approach to malware incident prevention should incorporate policy considerations, awareness programs for users and information technology (IT) staff, vulnerability and threat mitigation efforts, and defensive architecture considerations.

Organizations Should Ensure That Their Policies Address Prevention of Malware Incidents

An organization's policy statements should be used as the basis for additional malware prevention efforts, such as user and IT staff awareness, vulnerability mitigation, threat mitigation, and defensive architecture. If an organization does not state malware prevention considerations clearly in its policies, it is unlikely to perform malware prevention activities consistently and effectively throughout the organization. Malware prevention–related policy should be as general as possible to provide flexibility in policy implementation and to reduce the need for frequent policy updates, but should also be specific enough to make the intent and scope of the policy clear. Malware prevention–related policy should include provisions related to remote workers—both those using hosts controlled by the organization and those using hosts outside of the organization's control (e.g., contractor computers, employees' home computers, business partners' computers, mobile devices).

Organizations Should Incorporate Malware Incident Prevention and Handling into Their Awareness Programs

Organizations should implement awareness programs that include guidance to users on malware incident prevention. All users should be made aware of the ways that malware enters and infects hosts, the risks that malware poses, the inability of technical controls to prevent all incidents, and the importance of users in preventing incidents, with an emphasis on avoiding social engineering attacks. Awareness programs should also make users aware of policies and procedures that apply to malware incident handling, such as how to identify if a host may be infected, how to report a suspected incident, and what users might need to do to assist with incident handling. In addition, the organization should conduct awareness activities for IT staff involved in malware incident prevention and provide training on specific tasks.

Organizations Should Have Vulnerability Mitigation Capabilities to Help Prevent Malware Incidents

Organizations should have documented policy, processes, and procedures to mitigate known vulnerabilities that malware might exploit. Because a vulnerability usually can be mitigated through one or more methods, organizations should use an appropriate combination of techniques, including security automation technologies with security configuration checklists and patch management, and additional host hardening measures so that effective techniques are readily available for various types of vulnerabilities.

Organizations Should Have Threat Mitigation Capabilities to Assist in Containing Malware Incidents

Organizations should perform threat mitigation to detect and stop malware before it can affect its targets. The most commonly used malware threat mitigation technical control is antivirus software; organizations should deploy antivirus software on all hosts for which satisfactory antivirus software is available. Additional technical controls that are helpful for malware threat mitigation include intrusion prevention systems, firewalls, content filtering and inspection, and application whitelisting. The System and Information Integrity family of security controls in NIST Special Publication (SP) 800-53, *Recommended Security Controls for Federal Information Systems and Organizations*, recommends having malware protection mechanisms on various types of hosts, including workstations, servers, mobile computing devices, firewalls, email servers, web servers, and remote access servers.

Organizations Should Consider Using Defensive Architecture Methods to Reduce the Impact of Malware Incidents

No matter how rigorous vulnerability and threat mitigation efforts are, malware incidents will still occur. Organizations should consider altering the defensive architecture of their hosts' software to help mitigate those incidents that still occur. One technique is sandboxing, which is a security model where applications are run within a controlled environment that restricts what operations the applications can perform and isolates them from other applications. Another technique is browser separation, which involves using different web browsers for different types of website access (corporate applications, general access, etc.) Finally, segregation through virtualization techniques separate applications or operating systems from each other through the use of virtualization, such as having one OS instance for corporate applications and another OS instance for all other activity.

Organizations Should Have a Robust Incident Response Process Capability That Addresses Malware Incident Handling

As defined in NIST SP 800-61, *Computer Security Incident Handling Guide*, the incident response process has four main phases: preparation, detection and analysis, containment/eradication/recovery, and post-incident activity. Some major recommendations for malware incident handling, by phase or subphase, are as follows:

- **Preparation.** Organizations should perform preparatory measures to ensure that they can respond effectively to malware incidents. Recommended actions include—
  - Building and maintaining malware-related skills within the incident response team
  - Facilitating communication and coordination throughout the organization
  - Acquiring the necessary tools (hardware and software) and resources to assist in malware incident handling
- **Detection and Analysis.** Organizations should strive to detect and validate malware incidents rapidly to minimize the number of infected hosts and the amount of damage the organization sustains. Recommended actions include—
  - Analyzing any suspected malware incident and validating that malware is the cause. This includes identifying characteristics of the malware activity by examining detection sources, such as antivirus software, intrusion prevention systems, and security information and event management (SIEM) technologies.
  - Identifying which hosts are infected by the malware, so that the hosts can undergo the appropriate containment, eradication, and recovery actions. Identifying infected hosts is often complicated by the dynamic nature of malware and computing. Organizations should carefully consider host identification issues before a large-

scale malware incident occurs so that they are prepared to use multiple strategies for identifying infected hosts as part of their containment efforts. Organizations should select a sufficiently broad range of identification approaches and should develop procedures and technical capabilities to perform each selected approach effectively when a major malware incident occurs.
    - Prioritizing the handling of each incident based on NIST SP 800-61 guidelines and additional malware-specific criteria
    - Studying the behavior of malware by analyzing it either actively (executing the malware) or forensically (examining an infected host for evidence of malware)
- **Containment.** Malware incident containment has two major components: stopping the spread of malware and preventing further damage to hosts. Nearly every malware incident requires containment actions. In addressing an incident, it is important for an organization to decide which methods of containment to employ initially, early in the response. Organizations should have strategies and procedures in place for making containment-related decisions that reflect the level of risk acceptable to the organization. Containment strategies should support incident handlers in selecting the appropriate combination of containment methods based on the characteristics of a particular situation. Specific containment-related recommendations include the following:
    - It can be helpful to provide users with instructions on how to identify infections and what measures to take if a host is infected; however, organizations should not rely primarily on users for containing malware incidents.
    - If malware cannot be identified and contained by updated antivirus software, organizations should be prepared to use other security tools to contain it. Organizations should also be prepared to submit copies of unknown malware to their security software vendors for analysis, as well as contacting trusted parties such as incident response organizations and antivirus vendors when guidance is needed on handling new threats.
    - Organizations should be prepared to shut down or block services used by malware to contain an incident and should understand the consequences of doing so. Organizations should also be prepared to respond to problems caused by other organizations disabling their own services in response to a malware incident.

  - Organizations should be prepared to place additional temporary restrictions on network connectivity to contain a malware incident, such as suspending Internet access or physically disconnecting hosts from networks, recognizing the impact that the restrictions might have on organizational functions.
- **Eradication.** The primary goal of eradication is to remove malware from infected hosts. Because of the potential need for extensive eradication efforts, organizations should be prepared to use various combinations of eradication techniques simultaneously for different situations. Organizations should also consider performing awareness activities that set expectations for eradication and recovery efforts; these activities can be helpful in reducing the stress that major malware incidents can cause.
- **Recovery.** The two main aspects of recovery from malware incidents are restoring the functionality and data of infected hosts and removing temporary containment measures. Organizations should carefully consider possible worst-case scenarios and determine how recovery should be performed, including rebuilding compromised hosts from scratch or known good backups. Determining when to remove temporary containment measures, such as suspension of services or connectivity, is often a difficult decision during major malware incidents. Incident response teams should strive to keep containment measures in place until the estimated number of infected hosts and hosts vulnerable to infection is sufficiently low that subsequent incidents should be of little consequence. However, even though the incident response team should assess the risks of restoring services or connectivity, management ultimately should be responsible for determining what should be done based on the incident response team's recommendations and management's understanding of the business impact of maintaining the containment measures.
- **Post-Incident Activity.** Because the handling of malware incidents can be extremely expensive, it is particularly important for organizations to conduct a robust assessment of lessons learned after major malware incidents to prevent similar incidents from occurring. Capturing the lessons learned from the handling of such incidents should help an organization improve its incident handling capability and malware defenses, including identifying needed changes to security policy, software configurations, and malware detection and prevention software deployments.

1. INTRODUCTION

1.1. Purpose and Scope

This publication is intended to help a wide variety of organizations understand the threats posed by malware and mitigate the risks associated with malware incidents. In addition to providing background information on the major categories of malware, it provides practical, real-world guidance on preventing malware incidents and responding to malware incidents in an effective, efficient manner. The information presented in this publication is intended to be used as data points entered into a much larger risk management process. See the latest version of NIST SP 800-37, *Guide for Applying the Risk Management Framework to Federal Information Systems* for information on the basics of risk management.[1]

This publication is based on the assumption that the organization already has a general incident response program and capability in place. See the latest version of NIST SP 800-61, *Computer Security Incident Handling Guide* for more information on general incident response.[2] NIST SP 800-61 serves as the foundation for this publication.

1.2. Audience

This document has been created for computer security staff and program managers, technical support staff and managers, computer security incident response teams, and system and network administrators, who are responsible for preventing, preparing for, or responding to malware incidents.

1.3. Document Structure

The remainder of this guide is divided into three major sections. Section 2 defines, discusses, and compares the various categories of malware. Section 3 provides recommendations for preventing malware incidents through several layers of controls. Section 4 explains the malware incident response process, focusing on practical strategies for detection, containment, eradication, and recovery.

The guide also contains several appendices with supporting material. Appendices A and B contain a glossary and an acronym list, respectively.

Appendix C lists resources that can help readers gain a better understanding of malware, malware incident prevention, and malware incident handling.

2. Understanding Malware Threats

Malware, also known as malicious code, refers to a program that is covertly inserted into another program with the intent to destroy data, run destructive or intrusive programs, or otherwise compromise the confidentiality, integrity, or availability of the victim's data, applications, or operating system. Malware is the most common external threat to most hosts, causing widespread damage and disruption and necessitating extensive recovery efforts within most organizations.

This section provides basic information on various forms of malware. It defines common terminology that is used throughout the rest of the document, and it presents fundamental concepts of malware. It does not attempt to explain how these different types of malware work in detail, but rather it highlights the basic characteristics of each type of malware. This section first discusses attacker tools, which are often delivered to targeted hosts via malware, and malware toolkits, which are used by attackers to construct malware. The rest of the section examines forms of malware: traditional, phishing, web-based malware, and advanced persistent threats.

2.1. Forms of Malware

Malware has become the greatest external threat to most hosts, causing damage and requiring extensive recovery efforts within most organizations. The following are the classic categories of malware:

- **Viruses.** A virus self-replicates by inserting copies of itself into host programs or data files. Viruses are often triggered through user interaction, such as opening a file or running a program. Viruses can be divided into the following two subcategories:
  - **Compiled Viruses.** A compiled virus is executed by an operating system. Types of compiled viruses include file infector viruses, which attach themselves to executable programs; boot sector viruses, which infect the master boot records of hard drives or the boot sectors of removable media; and multipartite viruses, which

combine the characteristics of file infector and boot sector viruses.

- **Interpreted Viruses.** Interpreted viruses are executed by an application. Within this subcategory, macro viruses take advantage of the capabilities of applications' macro programming language to infect application documents and document templates, while scripting viruses infect scripts that are understood by scripting languages processed by services on the OS.

- **Worms.** A worm is a self-replicating, self-contained program that usually executes itself without user intervention. Worms are divided into two categories:
    - **Network Service Worms.** A network service worm takes advantage of a vulnerability in a network service to propagate itself and infect other hosts.
    - **Mass Mailing Worms.** A mass mailing worm is similar to an email-borne virus but is self-contained, rather than infecting an existing file.
- **Trojan Horses.** A Trojan horse is a self-contained, nonreplicating program that, while appearing to be benign, actually has a hidden malicious purpose. Trojan horses either replace existing files with malicious versions or add new malicious files to hosts. They often deliver other attacker tools to hosts.
- **Malicious Mobile Code.** Malicious mobile code is software with malicious intent that is transmitted from a remote host to a local host and then executed on the local host, typically without the user's explicit instruction. Popular languages for malicious mobile code include Java, ActiveX, JavaScript, and VBScript.
- **Blended Attacks.** A blended attack uses multiple infection or transmission methods. For example, a blended attack could combine the propagation methods of viruses and worms.

Many, if not most, instances of malware today are blended attacks. Current malware also relies heavily on *social engineering*, which is a general term for attackers trying to trick people into revealing sensitive information or performing certain actions, such as downloading and executing files that appear to be benign but are actually malicious. Because so many instances of malware have a variety of malware characteristics, the classic malware categories listed above (virus, worm, etc.) are considerably less useful than they used to be for malware incident handling. At one time, there were largely different procedures for handling incidents of each malware category; now there is largely one set of procedures for handling all malware incidents, thus nullifying the primary need for having categories.

Another problem with the classic categories is that newer forms of malware do not neatly fit into them. For example, in the growing trend of *web-based malware*, also known as drive-by-download, a user's web browsing is redirected to an infected website, often with little or no use of social engineering techniques. The infected website then attempts to exploit vulnerabilities on the user's host and ultimately to install rootkits or other attacker tools onto the host, thus compromising the host. Although the website is infected, its malware does not infect the user's host; rather, it functions as an attacker tool and installs other attacker tools on the host. Web-based malware is a blended attack of sorts, but its components do not map to the other malware categories.

The classic malware categories do not include *phishing*, which refers to use of deceptive computer-based means to trick individuals into disclosing sensitive personal information.[3] To perform a phishing attack, an attacker creates a website or email that looks as if it is from a well-known organization, such as an online business, credit card company, or financial institution. The fraudulent emails and websites are intended to deceive users into disclosing personal data, usually financial information. For example, phishers might seek usernames and passwords for online banking sites, as well as bank account numbers. Some phishing attacks overlap with web-based malware, because they install keystroke loggers or other attacker tools onto hosts to gather additional personal information.

Organizations should avoid expending substantial time and resources in categorizing each malware incident based on the types of categories expressed above.

2.2. Attacker Tools

Various types of attacker tools might be delivered to a host by malware. These tools allow attackers to have unauthorized access to or use of infected hosts and their data, or to launch additional attacks. Popular types of attacker tools are as follows:

- **Backdoors.** A backdoor is a malicious program that listens for commands on a certain TCP or UDP port. Most backdoors allow an attacker to perform a certain set of actions on a host, such as acquiring passwords or executing arbitrary commands. Types of backdoors include zombies (better known as bots), which are installed on a host to cause it to attack other hosts, and remote administration tools, which are installed on a host to enable a remote attacker to gain access to the host's functions and data as needed.
- **Keystroke Loggers.** A keystroke logger monitors and records keyboard use. Some require the attacker to retrieve the data from the host, whereas other loggers actively transfer the data to another host through email, file transfer, or other means.
- **Rootkits.** A rootkit is a collection of files that is installed on a host to alter its standard functionality in a malicious and stealthy way. A rootkit typically makes many changes to a host to hide the rootkit's existence, making it very difficult to determine that the rootkit is present and to identify what the rootkit has changed.
- **Web Browser Plug-Ins.** A web browser plug-in provides a way for certain types of content to be displayed or executed through a web browser. Malicious web browser plug-ins can monitor all use of a browser.
- **E-Mail Generators.** An email generating program can be used to create and send large quantities of email, such as malware and spam, to other hosts without the user's permission or knowledge.
- **Attacker Toolkits.** Many attackers use toolkits containing several different types of utilities and scripts that can be used to probe and attack hosts, such as packet sniffers, port scanners, vulnerability scanners, password crackers, and attack programs and scripts.

Because attacker tools can be detected by antivirus software, some people think of them as forms of malware. However, attacker tools have no infections capability on their own; they rely on malware or other attack mechanisms to install them onto target hosts. Strictly speaking, attacker tools are not malware, but because they are so closely tied to malware and often detected and removed using the same tools, attacker tools will be covered where appropriate throughout this publication.

2.3. The Nature of Today's Malware

The characteristic of today's malware that most distinguishes it from previous generations of malware is its degree of customization. It has become trivial for attackers to create their own malware by acquiring malware toolkits, such as Zeus, SpyEye, and Poison Ivy, and customizing the malware produced by those toolkits to meet their individual needs. Many of these toolkits are available for purchase, while others are open source, and most have user-friendly interfaces that make it simple for unskilled attackers to create customized, high-capability malware.

Here's an example of what a malware toolkit can do, illustrated by how the resulting attack works

1. The toolkit sends spam to users, attempting to trick them into visiting a particular website.
2. Users visit the website, which has malicious content provided by the toolkit.
3. The website infects the users' computers with Trojan horses (provided by the toolkit) by exploiting vulnerabilities in the computers' operating systems.
4. The Trojan horses install attacker tools, such as keystroke loggers and rootkits (provided by the toolkit).

Many attackers further customize their malware by tailoring each instance of malware to a particular person or small group of people. For example, many attackers harvest information through social networks, then use that affiliation and relationship information to craft superior social engineering attacks.

Other examples are the frequent use of *spear phishing* attacks, which are targeted phishing attacks, and *whaling* attacks, which are spear phishing attacks targeted at executives and other individuals with access to information of particular interest or value.

Malware customization causes significant problems for malware detection, because it greatly increases the variety of malware that antivirus software and other security controls need to detect and block. When attackers are capable of sending a unique attack to each potential victim, it should not be surprising that largely signature-based security controls, such as antivirus software, cannot keep up with them. Mitigation involves a defense in depth approach, using several different detection techniques to increase the odds that at least one of them can detect the malicious behavior of the customized malware.

In addition to customization, another important characteristic of today's malware is its stealthy nature. Unlike most malware several years ago, which tended to be easy to notice, much of today's malware is specifically designed to quietly, slowly spread to other hosts, gathering information over extended periods of time and eventually leading to exfiltration of sensitive data and other negative impacts. The term *advanced persistent threats* (APTs) is generally used to refer to such types of malware. The attack scenario outlined in the above box could be an example of an advanced persistent threat if it was stealthy. APTs may conduct surveillance for weeks, months, or even years, potentially causing extensive damage to an organization with just one compromise. APTs are also notoriously difficult to remove from hosts, often requiring the host's operating system and applications to be reinstalled and all data restored from known good backups.

In summary, today's malware is often harder to detect, more damaging, and harder to remove than previous generations of malware. And there is no indication that this evolution is at an end. When today's hardest malware problems become routine to address, expect new challenges to emerge.

3. Malware Incident Prevention

This section presents recommendations for preventing malware incidents within an organization. The main elements of prevention are policy, awareness, vulnerability mitigation, threat mitigation, and defensive architecture. Ensuring that policies address malware prevention provides a basis for implementing preventive controls. Establishing and maintaining general malware awareness programs for all users, as well as specific awareness training for the IT staff directly involved in malware prevention–related activities, are critical to reducing the number of incidents that occur through human error. Expending effort on vulnerability mitigation can eliminate some possible attack vectors. Implementing a combination of threat mitigation techniques and tools, such as antivirus software and firewalls, can prevent threats from successfully attacking hosts and networks. Also, using defensive architectures such as sandboxing, browser separation, and segregation through virtualization can reduce the impact of compromises. Sections 3.1 through 3.5 address each of these areas in detail and explain that organizations should implement guidance from each category of recommendations to create an effective layered defense against malware.

When planning an approach to malware prevention, organizations should be mindful of the attack vectors that are most likely to be used currently and in the near future.[4] They should also consider how well- controlled their hosts are (e.g., managed environment, non-managed environment); this has significant bearing on the effectiveness of various preventive approaches. In addition, organizations should incorporate existing capabilities, such as antivirus software deployments and patch management programs, into their malware prevention efforts. However, organizations should be aware that no matter how much effort they put into malware incident prevention, incidents will still occur (e.g., previously unknown types of threats, human error). For this reason, as described in Section 4, organizations should have robust malware incident handling capabilities to limit the damage that malware can cause and restore data and services efficiently.

3.1. Policy

Organizations should ensure that their policies address prevention of malware incidents. These policy statements should be used as the basis for additional malware prevention efforts, such as user and IT staff awareness, vulnerability mitigation, threat mitigation, and defensive architecture (described in Sections 3.2 through 3.5, respectively). If an organization does not state malware prevention considerations clearly in its policies, it is unlikely to perform malware prevention activities consistently and effectively throughout the organization. Malware prevention–related policy should be as general as possible to provide flexibility in policy implementation and to reduce the need for frequent policy updates, but also specific enough to make the intent and scope of the policy clear. Although some organizations have separate malware policies, many malware prevention considerations belong in other policies, such as acceptable use policies, so a separate malware policy might duplicate some of the content of other policies.[5] Malware prevention–related policy should include provisions related to remote workers—both those using hosts controlled by the organization and those using hosts outside of the organization's control (e.g., contractor computers, employees' home computers, business partners' computers, mobile devices).

Common malware prevention–related policy considerations include the following:[6]

- Requiring the scanning of media from outside of the organization for malware before they can be used
- Requiring that email file attachments be scanned before they are opened
- Prohibiting the sending or receipt of certain types of files (e.g., .exe files) via email
- Restricting or prohibiting the use of unnecessary software, such as user applications that are often used to transfer malware (e.g., personal use of external instant messaging and file sharing services)
- Restricting the use of removable media (e.g., flash drives), particularly on hosts that are at high risk of infection, such as publicly accessible kiosks
- Specifying which types of preventive software (e.g., antivirus software, content filtering software) are required for each type of host (e.g., email server, web server, laptop, smart phone) and application (e.g., email client, web browser), and listing the high-level requirements for configuring and maintaining the software (e.g., software update frequency, host scan scope and frequency)
- Restricting or prohibiting the use of organization-issued and/or personally-owned mobile devices on the organization's networks and for telework/remote access.

3.2. Awareness

An effective awareness program explains proper rules of behavior for use of an organization's IT hosts and information. Accordingly, awareness programs should include guidance to users on malware incident prevention, which can help reduce the frequency and severity of malware incidents. All users should be made aware of the ways in which malware enters and infects hosts; the risks that malware poses; the inability of technical controls to prevent all incidents; and the importance of users in preventing incidents, with an emphasis on avoiding social engineering attacks (as discussed below). In addition, the organization's awareness program should cover the malware incident prevention considerations in the organization's policies and procedures, as described in Section 3.1, as well as generally recommended practices for avoiding malware incidents. Examples of such practices are as follows:

- Not opening suspicious emails or email attachments, clicking on hyperlinks, etc. from unknown or known senders, or visiting websites that are likely to contain malicious content
- Not clicking on suspicious web browser popup windows
- Not opening files with file extensions that are likely to be associated with malware (e.g., .bat, .com, .exe, .pif, .vbs)
- Not disabling malware security control mechanisms (e.g., antivirus software, content filtering software, reputation software, personal firewall)
- Not using administrator-level accounts for regular host operation
- Not downloading or executing applications from untrusted sources.

As described in Section 4, organizations should also make users aware of policies and procedures that apply to malware incident handling, such as how to identify if a host may be infected, how to report a suspected incident, and what users might need to do to assist with incident handling (e.g., updating antivirus software, scanning hosts for malware). Users should be made aware of how the organization will communicate notices of major malware incidents and given a way to verify the authenticity of all such notices. In addition, users should be aware of changes that might be temporarily made to the environment to contain an incident, such as disconnecting infected hosts from networks.

As part of awareness activities, organizations should educate their users on the social engineering techniques that are employed to trick users into disclosing information. Examples of recommendations for avoiding phishing attacks and other forms of social engineering include:

- Never reply to email requests for financial or personal information. Instead, contact the person or the organization at the legitimate phone number or website. Do not use the contact information provided in the email, and do not click on any attachments or hyperlinks in the email.
- Do not provide passwords, PINs, or other access codes in response to emails or unsolicited popup windows. Only enter such information into the legitimate website or application.
- Do not open suspicious email file attachments, even if they come from known senders. If an unexpected attachment is received, contact the sender (preferably by a method other than email, such as phone) to confirm that the attachment is legitimate.

- Do not respond to any suspicious or unwanted emails. (Asking to have an email address removed from a malicious party's mailing list confirms the existence and active use of that email address, potentially leading to additional attack attempts.)

Although user awareness programs are increasingly important to help reduce the frequency and severity of social engineering-driven malware incidents, the impact of these programs is still typically not as great as that of the technical controls described in Sections 3.3 through 3.5 for malware incident prevention. An organization should not rely on user awareness as its primary method of preventing malware incidents; instead, the awareness program should supplement the technical controls to provide additional protection against incidents.

The awareness program for users should also serve as the foundation for awareness activities for the IT staff involved in malware incident prevention, such as security, system, and network administrators. All IT staff members should have some basic level of awareness regarding malware prevention, and individuals should be trained in the malware prevention–related tasks that pertain to their areas of responsibility. In addition, on an ongoing basis, some IT staff members (most likely, some members of the security or incident response teams) should receive and review bulletins on types of new malware threats, assess the likely risk to the organization, and inform the necessary IT staff members of the new threat so that incidents can be prevented. IT staff awareness activities related to malware incident handling are discussed in Section 4.

3.3. Vulnerability Mitigation

As described in Section 2, malware often attacks hosts by exploiting vulnerabilities in operating systems, services, and applications. Consequently, mitigating vulnerabilities is very important to the prevention of malware incidents, particularly when malware is released shortly after the announcement of a new vulnerability, or even before a vulnerability is publicly acknowledged. A vulnerability can usually be mitigated by one or more methods, such as applying patches to update the software or reconfiguring the software (e.g., disabling a vulnerable service). Because of the challenges that vulnerability mitigation presents, including handling the continual discovery of new vulnerabilities, organizations should have documented policy, processes, and procedures for vulnerability mitigation.

Organizations should consider using security automation technologies with OS and application configuration checklists to help administrators secure hosts consistently and effectively. Security automation technologies can use checklists to apply configuration settings that improve the default level of security and to continuously monitor the hosts' settings to verify that they are still in compliance with the checklist settings.[7] Organizations should also consider using security automation technologies for OS and application patch management—to identify, acquire, distribute, and install security-related patches so as to mitigate vulnerabilities that the patches address.[8]

In terms of security configurations, organizations should use sound host hardening principles. For example, organizations should follow the principle of least privilege, which refers to configuring hosts to provide only the minimum necessary rights to the appropriate users, processes, and hosts. Least privilege can be helpful in preventing malware incidents, because malware often requires administrator-level privileges to exploit vulnerabilities successfully. If an incident does occur, prior application of least privilege might minimize the amount of damage that the malware can cause. Organizations should also implement other host hardening measures that can further reduce the possibility of malware incidents, such as the following:

- Disabling or removing unneeded services (particularly network services), which are additional vectors that malware can use to spread
- Eliminating unsecured file shares, which are a common way for malware to spread
- Removing or changing default usernames and passwords for OSs and applications, which could be used by malware to gain unauthorized access to hosts
- Disabling automatic execution of binaries and scripts, including AutoRun on Windows hosts
- Changing the default file associations for file types that are most frequently used by malware but not by users (e.g., .pif, .vbs) so that such files are not run automatically if users attempt to open them.

Host hardening should also include applications, such as email clients, web browsers, and word processors, that are frequently targeted by malware. Organizations should disable unneeded features and capabilities from these applications, particularly those that are commonly exploited by malware, to limit the possible attack vectors for malware. One example is the use of macro languages by word processors and spreadsheets; most common applications with macro capabilities offer macro security features that permit macros only from trusted locations or prompt the user to approve or reject each attempt to run a macro, thus reducing the chance of macro-induced malware infection. Another example is preventing software installation within web browsers by configuring browsers to prohibit plug-in installation or to prompt users to approve the installation of each plug-in.

Being able to alter application configuration settings quickly can be very beneficial in remediating vulnerabilities very quickly, including temporary remediation measures. For example, a configuration change could disable a vulnerable service temporarily while the service's vendor prepares and releases a patch that permanently fixes the vulnerability. Once the patch is available and deployed, the organization can reverse the configuration change to reactivate the no longer vulnerable service. Organizations should consider in advance how configuration settings could be changed in response to a malware emergency and establish and maintain appropriate procedures.

3.4. Threat Mitigation

Organizations should perform threat mitigation to detect and stop malware before it can affect its targets. Even if virtually all vulnerabilities in a host have been mitigated, threat mitigation is still critically important—for example, for stopping instances of malware that do not exploit vulnerabilities, such as attacks that rely on social engineering methods to trick users into running malicious files. Threat mitigation is also critical for situations where a major new threat is likely to attack an organization soon and the organization does not have an acceptable vulnerability mitigation option. For example, there might not be a patch available for a new vulnerability.

This section describes several types of security tools that can mitigate malware threats: antivirus software, intrusion prevention systems (IPS), firewalls, content filtering/inspection, and application whitelisting. For each of these categories, the section also describes typical features, the types of malware and attack vectors the tools address, and the methods they use to detect and stop malware. Recommendations and guidance for implementing, configuring, and maintaining the tools are also provided, as well as explanations of the tools' shortcomings and the ways in which they complement other tools. In addition, the section discusses client and server application settings that can be helpful in mitigating threats.

3.4.1. Antivirus Software

Antivirus software is the most commonly used technical control for malware threat mitigation. There are many brands of antivirus software, with most providing similar protection through the following recommended capabilities:

- Scanning critical host components such as startup files and boot records.
- Watching real-time activities on hosts to check for suspicious activity; a common example is scanning all email attachments for known malware as emails are sent and received. Antivirus software should be configured to perform real-time scans of each file as it is downloaded, opened, or executed, which is known as *on-access scanning*.
- Monitoring the behavior of common applications, such as email clients, web browsers, and instant messaging software. Antivirus software should monitor activity involving the applications most likely to be used to infect hosts or spread malware to other hosts.
- Scanning files for known malware. Antivirus software on hosts should be configured to scan all hard drives regularly to identify any file system infections and, optionally, depending on organization security needs, to scan removable media inserted into the host before allowing its use. Users should also be able to launch a scan manually as needed, which is known as *on-demand scanning*.
- Identifying common types of malware as well as attacker tools.
- *Disinfecting* files, which refers to removing malware from within a file, and *quarantining* files, which means that files containing malware are stored in isolation for future disinfection or examination. Disinfecting a file is generally preferable to quarantining it because the malware is removed and the original file restored; however, many infected files cannot be disinfected. Accordingly, antivirus software should be configured to attempt to disinfect infected files and to either quarantine or delete files that cannot be disinfected.

Organizations should use both host-based and network-based antivirus scanning. Organizations should deploy antivirus software on all hosts for which satisfactory antivirus software is available. Antivirus software should be installed as soon after OS installation as possible and then updated with the latest signatures and antivirus software patches (to eliminate any known vulnerabilities in the antivirus software itself). The antivirus software should then perform a complete scan of the host to identify any potential infections. To support the security of the host, the antivirus software should be configured and maintained properly so that it continues to be effective at detecting and stopping malware. Antivirus software is most effective when its signatures are fully up-to-date. Accordingly, antivirus software should be kept current with the latest signature and software updates to improve malware detection.

Organizations should use centrally managed antivirus software that is controlled and monitored regularly by antivirus administrators, who are also typically responsible for acquiring, testing, approving, and delivering antivirus signature and software updates throughout the organization. Users should not be able to disable or delete antivirus software from their hosts, nor should they be able to alter critical settings. Antivirus administrators should perform continuous monitoring to confirm that hosts are using current antivirus software and that the software is configured properly. Implementing all of these recommendations should strongly support an organization in having a strong and consistent antivirus deployment across the organization.

A possible measure for improving malware prevention is to use multiple antivirus products for key hosts, such as email servers. For example, one antivirus vendor might have a new signature available several hours before another vendor, or an organization might have an operational issue with a particular signature update. Another possibility is that an antivirus product itself might contain an exploitable vulnerability; having an alternative product available in such cases could provide protection until the issue with the primary product has been resolved. Because running multiple antivirus products on a single host simultaneously is likely to cause conflicts between the products, if multiple products are used concurrently, they should be installed on separate hosts. For example, one antivirus product could be used on perimeter email servers and another on internal email servers. This could provide more effective detection of new threats, but also would necessitate increased administration and training, as well as additional hardware and software costs.

Although antivirus software has become a necessity for malware incident prevention, it is not possible for antivirus software to stop all malware incidents. As discussed previously in this section, antivirus software does not excel at stopping previously unknown threats. Antivirus software products detect malware primarily by looking for certain characteristics of known instances of malware. This is highly effective for identifying known malware, but is not so effective at detecting the highly customized, tailored malware increasingly being used.

3.4.2. Intrusion Prevention Systems

Network-based intrusion prevention systems (IPS) perform packet sniffing and analyze network traffic to identify and stop suspicious activity.[9] Network-based IPS products are typically deployed *inline*, which means that the software acts like a network firewall. It receives packets, analyzes them, and allows acceptable packets to pass through. The network-based IPS architecture allows some attacks to be detected on networks before they reach their intended targets. Most network-based IPS products use a combination of attack signatures and analysis of network and application protocols, which means that they compare network activity for frequently attacked applications (e.g., email servers, web servers) to expected behavior to identify potentially malicious activity.

Network-based IPS products are used to detect many types of malicious activity besides malware, and typically can detect only a few instances of malware by default, such as recent major worms. However, some IPS products are highly customizable, allowing administrators to create and deploy attack signatures for many major new malware threats in a matter of minutes. Although there are risks in doing this, such as a poorly written signature triggering false positives that block benign activity inadvertently, a custom signature can block a new malware threat hours before antivirus signatures become available. Network-based IPS products can be effective at stopping specific known threats, such as network service worms, and email–borne malware with easily recognizable characteristics (e.g., subject, attachment filename).

Another form of IPS, known as a *network behavior analysis (NBA) system*, attempts to stop attacks by identifying unusual network traffic flows. Although these products are primarily intended to stop distributed denial of service (DDoS) attacks against an organization, they can also be used to identify worm activity and other forms of malware, as well as use of attacker tools such as backdoors and email generators. An NBA system typically works by monitoring normal network traffic patterns, including which hosts communicate with each other using which protocols, and the typical and peak volumes of activity, to establish baselines. The software then monitors network activity to identify significant deviations from the baselines. If malware causes a particularly high volume of network traffic or uses network or application protocols that are not typically seen, an NBA system should be able to detect and, if deployed inline, block the activity. Another way of limiting some malware incidents is by configuring network devices to limit the maximum amount of bandwidth that can be used by particular hosts or services. Also, some types of network monitoring software can detect and report significant deviations from expected network activity, although this software typically cannot specifically label the activity as malware-related or block it.

Host-based IFS products are similar in principle and purpose to other IPSs, except that a host-based IPS product monitors the characteristics of a single host and the events occurring within that host. Examples of activity that might be monitored by host-based IPSs include network traffic, host logs, running processes, file access and modification, and host and application configuration changes. Host-based IPS products often use a combination of attack signatures and knowledge of expected or typical behavior to identify known and unknown attacks on hosts. For example, host-based IPS products that monitor attempted changes to files can be effective at detecting viruses attempting to infect files and Trojan horses attempting to replace files, as well as the use of attacker tools, such as rootkits, that often are delivered by malware. If a host-based IPS product monitors the host's network traffic, it offers detection capabilities similar to a network-based IPS's.

See NIST SP 800-94, *Guide to Intrusion Detection and Prevention Systems (IDPS)* for more information on IPSs.[10]

3.4.3. Firewalls

A *network firewall* is a device deployed between networks to restrict which types of traffic can pass from one network to another. A *host-based firewall* is a piece of software running on a single host that can restrict incoming and outgoing network activity for that host only. Both types of firewalls can be useful for preventing malware incidents. Organizations should configure their firewalls with *deny by default* rulesets, meaning that the firewalls deny all incoming traffic that is not expressly permitted. With such rulesets in place, malware could not spread using services deemed unnecessary to the organization.[11] Organizations should also restrict outgoing traffic to the degree feasible, with a focus on preventing the use of prohibited services commonly used by malware.

When a major new malware threat targeting a network service is impending, organizations might need to rely on firewalls to prevent an incident. To prepare for worst-case situations, organizations should be ready to add or change firewall rules quickly to prevent a network service–based malware incident. Firewall rules might also be helpful in stopping malware that relies on particular IP addresses, such as a worm that downloads Trojan horses from one of five external hosts. Adding a rule that blocks all activity involving the external hosts' IP addresses could prevent the Trojan horses from reaching the organization.

More information on firewalls is available from NIST SP 800-41 Revision 1, *Guidelines on Firewalls and Firewall Policy* (http://csrc.nist.gov /publications/PubsSPs.html#800-41).

3.4.4. Content Filtering/Inspection

Organizations should use content inspection and filtering technologies for stopping email-based malware threats. Organizations should use spam filtering technologies to reduce the amount of spam that reaches users.[12] Spam is often used for malware delivery, particularly phishing attacks, so reducing spam should lead to a corresponding decline in spam-triggered malware incidents. Organizations should also consider configuring their email servers and clients to block attachments with file extensions that are associated with malicious code (e.g., .pif, .vbs), and suspicious file extension combinations (e.g., .txt.vbs, .htm.exe). However, this might also inadvertently block legitimate activity. Some organizations alter suspicious email attachment file extensions so that a recipient would have to save the attachment and rename it before running it, which can be a good compromise between functionality and security.

Organizations should also use content inspection and filtering technologies for stopping web-based malware threats. Web content filtering software has several ways of doing this; although it is typically thought of as preventing access to materials that are inappropriate for the workplace, it may also contain blacklist and reputation information (see below). It can also block undesired file types, such as by file extension or by mobile code type. For particularly high security situations, organizations should consider restricting which types of mobile code (such as unsigned ActiveX) may or may not be used from various sources (e.g., internal servers, external servers).

Organizations should also block undesired web browser popup windows, as a form of content filtering. Some popup windows are crafted to look like legitimate system message boxes or websites, and can trick users into going to phony websites, including sites used for phishing, or authorizing changes to their hosts, among other malicious actions. Most web browsers can block popup windows, and third-party popup blockers are also available.

Both email and web content filtering should use real-time blacklists, reputation services, and other similar mechanisms whenever feasible to avoid accepting content from known or likely malicious hosts and domains. These mechanisms use a variety of techniques to identify certain IP addresses, domain names, or URIs as being probably malicious or probably benign. Real-time blacklists tend to be based on observed malware activity, while reputation services may be based on user opinions or on automated analysis of websites, emails, etc. without necessarily detecting malware. Because the fidelity and accuracy of these mechanisms varies widely from one implementation to another, organizations should carefully evaluate any real-time blacklists, reputation services, or other similar mechanisms before deploying them into production environments to minimize disruption to operations.

3.4.5. Application Whitelisting

Application whitelisting technologies, also known as application control programs, are used to specify which applications are authorized for use on a host. Most application whitelisting technologies can be run in two modes: audit and enforcement. In enforcement mode, the technology generally prohibits all applications that are not in the whitelist from being executed. In audit mode, the technology logs all instances of non-whitelisted applications being run on the host, but does not act to stop them. The tradeoff between enforcement mode and audit mode is simple; using enforcement mode will stop malware from executing, but it may also prevent benign applications not included on the whitelist from being run. Organizations deploying application whitelisting technologies should consider first deploying them in audit mode, so as to identify any necessary applications missing from the whitelist, before reconfiguring them for enforcement mode. Running application whitelisting technologies in audit mode is analogous to intrusion detection software without intrusion prevention capabilities; it can be useful after an infection occurs to determine which hosts were affected, but it has no ability to prevent infections.

Organizations with high security needs or high-risk environments should consider the use of application whitelisting technologies for their managed hosts. Application whitelisting technologies are built into many operating systems and are also available through third-party utilities.

3.5. Defensive Architecture

No matter how rigorous vulnerability and threat mitigation efforts are, malware incidents will still occur. This section describes four types of complementary methods that organizations should consider using to alter the defensive architecture of a host's software so as to reduce the impact of incidents: BIOS protection, sandboxing, browser separation, and segregation through virtualization.

3.5.1. BIOS Protection

Unauthorized modification of BIOS firmware by malicious software constitutes a significant threat because of the BIOS's unique and privileged position within the PC architecture. A malicious BIOS modification could be part of a sophisticated, targeted attack on an organization—either a permanent denial of service (if the BIOS is corrupted) or a persistent malware presence (if the BIOS is implanted with malware). The move from conventional BIOS implementations to implementations based on the Unified Extensible Firmware Interface (UEFI) may make it easier for malware to target the BIOS in a widespread fashion, as these BIOS implementations are based on a common specification.[13] NIST Special Publication 800-147[14] provides guidelines for significantly improving BIOS protection and integrity, which is a necessary foundation for the other host-based methods.

3.5.2. Sandboxing

Sandboxing refers to a security model where applications are run within a sandbox—a controlled environment that restricts what operations the applications can perform and that isolates them from other applications running on the same host. In a sandbox security model, typically only authorized "safe" operations may be performed within the sandbox; the sandbox prohibits applications within the sandbox from performing any other operations. The sandbox also restricts access to system resources, such as memory and the file system, to keep the sandbox's applications isolated from the host's other applications.

Sandboxing provides several benefits in terms of malware incident prevention and handling. By limiting the operations available, it can prevent malware from performing some or all of the malicious actions it is attempting to execute; this could prevent the malware from succeeding or reduce the damage it causes. And the sandboxing environment—the isolation—can further reduce the impact of the malware by restricting what information and functions the malware can access. Another benefit of sandboxing is that the sandbox itself can be reset to a known good state every time it is initialized.

3.5.3. Browser Separation

Multiple brands of Web browsers (e.g., Microsoft Internet Explorer, Mozilla Firefox, Apple Safari, Google Chrome, Opera) can be installed on a single host. Accessing Web sites containing malicious content is one of the most common ways for hosts to be attacked, such as malicious plug-ins being installed within a browser. To reduce the impact of such attacks, users can use one brand of browser for corporate applications and another brand of browser for all other website access. This separates the sensitive corporate data within one browser from the data within the other browser, providing better protection for the corporate data (although this alone cannot adequately secure browser data) and reducing the likelihood that malware encountered during general web browsing will affect corporate applications. Having a separate brand of browser for corporate applications also allows that browser to be secured more tightly, such as disabling all forms of mobile code (e.g., Java, ActiveX) that are not required for the specified applications.

3.5.4. Segregation Through Virtualization

Browser separation essentially segregates web browsers from each other. Virtualization[15] can be used to segregate applications or operating systems from each other, with much more rigor than simple browser separation can provide. For example, an organization could have one OS instance for corporate applications and another OS instance for all other activities, including web browsing. Each OS instance is a known-good virtualized image that contains the appropriate applications and is secured accordingly. The user loads these virtualized images and does their work within these guest OS images, not directly on the host OS itself. A compromise occurring within one image will not affect the other image unless the compromise involves the virtualization software itself. Another benefit is that every time an image is restarted, it can be reloaded from the known-good image, ensuring that any compromises occurring within the image are eradicated.

An alternative strategy, more usable but less secure, is to use a guest OS for more risky behavior (such as general web browsing) and the host OS for corporate applications. This helps to isolate the riskier activities from the other activities on the host. The host OS can be restricted to only whitelisted applications (see Section 3.4.5) to prevent unauthorized applications from being run within it.

4. MALWARE INCIDENT RESPONSE

As defined in NIST SP 800-61, *Computer Security Incident Handling Guide,* the incident response process has four major phases: preparation, detection and analysis, containment/eradication/recovery, and post-incident activity. Figure 4-1 displays this incident response life cycle. This section of the guide builds on the concepts of SP 800-61 by providing additional details about responding to malware incidents.[16]

The initial phase of malware incident response involves performing preparatory activities, such as developing malware-specific incident handling procedures and training programs for incident response teams. As described in Section 3, the preparation phase also involves using policy, awareness activities, vulnerability mitigation, and security tools to reduce the number of malware incidents. Despite these measures, residual risk will inevitably persist, and no solution is foolproof. Detection of malware infections is thus necessary to alert the organization whenever incidents occur. Early detection is particularly important for malware incidents because they are more likely than other types of incidents to increase their impact over time, so faster detection and handling can help reduce the number of infected hosts and the damage done.

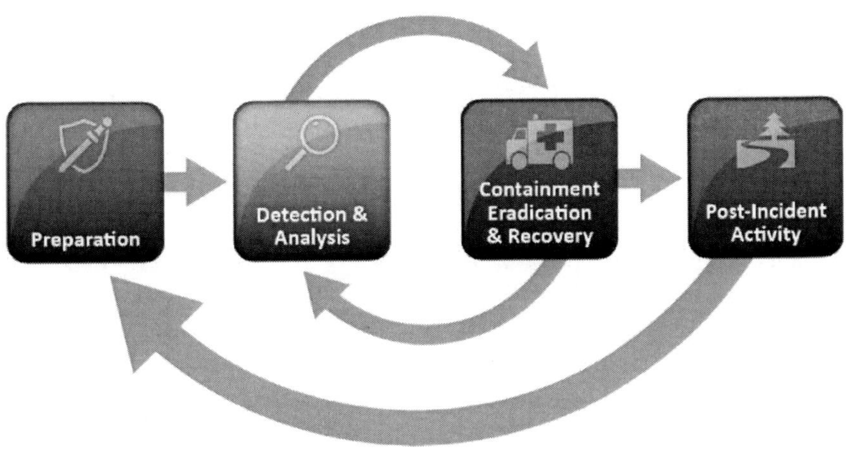

Figure 4-1. Incident Response Life Cycle.

For each incident, the organization should act appropriately, based on the severity of the incident, to mitigate its impact by containing it, eradicating infections, and ultimately recovering from the incident. The organization may need to jump back to the detection and analysis phase during containment, eradication, and recovery—for example, to check for additional infections that have occurred since the original detection was done. After an incident has been handled, the organization should issue a report that details the cause and cost of the incident and the steps the organization should take to prevent future incidents and to prepare more effectively to handle incidents that do occur.

This section of the document focuses on those aspects of incident handling that are specific to malware incidents.

4.1. Preparation

Organizations should perform preparatory measures to ensure that they are capable of responding effectively to malware incidents. Sections 4.1.1 through 4.1.3 describe several recommended preparatory measures, including building and maintaining malware-related skills within the incident response team, facilitating communication and coordination throughout the organization, and acquiring necessary tools and resources.

4.1.1. Building and Maintaining Malware-Related Skills

In addition to standard incident response team skills as described in NIST SP 800-61, all malware incident handlers should have a solid understanding of how each major category of malware infects hosts and spreads. Also, incident handlers should be familiar with the organization's implementations and configurations of malware detection tools so that they are better able to analyze supporting data and identify the characteristics of threats. Incident handlers doing in-depth malware analysis should have strong skills in that area and be familiar with the numerous tools for malware analysis, as described in Section 4.2.4.

Malware incident handlers should keep abreast of the ever-evolving landscape of malware threats and technology. Besides conducting malware-related training and exercises, organizations should also seek other ways of building and maintaining skills. One possibility is to have incident handlers temporarily work as antivirus engineers or administrators so that they can gain new technical skills and become more familiar with antivirus staff procedures and practices.

4.1.2. Facilitating Communication and Coordination

One of the most common problems during malware incident handling is poor communication and coordination. Anyone involved in an incident, including users, can inadvertently cause additional problems because of a limited view or understanding of the situation. To improve communication and coordination, an organization should designate in advance a few individuals or a small team to be responsible for coordinating the organization's responses to malware incidents. The coordinator's primary goal is to maintain situational awareness by gathering all pertinent information, making decisions that are in the best interests of the organization, and communicating pertinent information and decisions to all relevant parties in a timely manner. For malware incidents, the relevant parties often include end users, who might be given instructions on how to avoid infecting their hosts, how to recognize the signs of an infection, and what to do if a host appears to be infected. The coordinator also needs to provide technical guidance and instructions to all staff assisting with containment, eradication, and recovery efforts, as well as giving management regular updates on the status of the response and the current and likely future impact of the incident. Another possible role for the coordinator is interacting with external parties, such as other incident response teams facing similar malware issues.

Organizations should also establish a point of contact for answering questions about the legitimacy of malware alerts. Many organizations use the IT help desk as the initial point of contact and give help desk agents access to sources of information on real malware threats and virus hoaxes so that they can quickly determine the legitimacy of an alert and provide users with guidance on what to do. Organizations should caution users not to forward malware alerts to others without first confirming that the alerts are legitimate.

4.1.3. Acquiring Tools and Resources

Organizations should also ensure that they have the necessary tools (hardware and software) and resources to assist in malware incident handling. See Section 4.2.4 for more information on malware analysis toolkits, systems, and other related resources.

4.2. Detection and Analysis

Organizations should strive to detect and validate malware incidents rapidly to minimize the number of infected hosts and the amount of damage the organization sustains. Because malware can take many forms and be distributed through many means, there are many possible signs of a malware incident and many locations within an organization where the signs might be recorded or observed. It sometimes takes considerable analysis, requiring extensive technical knowledge and experience, to confirm that an incident has been caused by malware, particularly if the malware threat is new and unknown. After malware incident detection and validation, incident handlers should determine the type, extent, and magnitude of the problem as quickly as possible so that the response to the incident can be given the appropriate priority. Sections 4.2.1 through 4.2.4 provide guidance on identifying the characteristics of incidents, identifying infected hosts, prioritizing incident response efforts, and analyzing malware, respectively.

4.2.1. Identifying Malware Incident Characteristics

Because no indicator is completely reliable—even antivirus software might miscategorize benign activity as malicious—incident handlers need to analyze any suspected malware incident and validate that malware is the cause. In some cases, such as a massive, organization-wide infection, validation may be unnecessary because the nature of the incident is obvious. The goal is for incident handlers to be as certain as feasible that an incident is caused by malware and to have a basic understanding of the type of malware threat responsible, such as a worm or a Trojan horse. If the source of the incident cannot easily be confirmed, it is often better to respond as if it were caused by malware and to alter response efforts if it is later determined that malware is not involved. Waiting for conclusive evidence of malware might have a serious negative impact on response efforts and significantly increase the damage sustained by the organization.

As part of the analysis and validation process, incident handlers typically identify characteristics of the malware activity by examining detection sources. Understanding the activity's characteristics is very helpful in assigning an appropriate priority to the incident response efforts and planning effective containment, eradication, and recovery activities. Incident handlers should collaborate with security administrators in advance to identify data sources that can aid in detecting malware information and to understand what types of information each data source may record. In addition to the obvious sources of data, such as antivirus software, intrusion detection system (IDS), and security information and event management (SIEM) technologies, incident handlers should be aware of and use secondary sources as appropriate. See

Section 4.2 for more information on possible sources of malware characteristic information.

Once incident handlers have reviewed detection source data and identified characteristics of the malware, the handlers could search for those characteristics in antivirus vendors' malware databases and identify which instance of malware is the most likely cause. If the malware has been known for some time, it is likely that antivirus vendors will have a substantial amount of information on it, such as the following:

- Malware category (e.g., virus, worm, Trojan horse)
- Services, ports, protocols, etc. that are attacked
- Vulnerabilities that are exploited (e.g., software flaws, misconfigurations, social engineering)
- Malicious filenames, sizes, content, and other metadata (e.g., email subjects, web URLs)
- Which versions of operating systems, devices, applications, etc., may be affected
- How the malware affects the infected host, including the names and locations of affected files, altered configuration settings, installed backdoor ports, etc.
- How the malware propagates and how to approach containment
- How to remove the malware from the host.

Unfortunately, the newest threats might not be included in malware databases for several hours or days, depending on the relative importance of the threat, and highly customized threats might not be included in malware databases at all. Therefore, incident handlers may need to consult other sources of information. One option is using public security mailing lists, which might contain first-hand accounts of malware incidents; however, such reports are often incomplete or inaccurate, so incident handlers should validate any information obtained from these sources. Another potentially valuable source of malware characteristic information is peers at other organizations. Other organizations may have already been affected and gathered data on the threat. Establishing and maintaining good relationships with peers at other organizations that face similar problems can be advantageous for all involved. An alternative source of information is self-discovery by performing malware analysis (see Section 4.2.4). This is particularly important if the malware is highly customized; there may be no other way of getting details for the malware other than doing a hands-on analysis.

4.2.2. Identifying Infected Hosts

Identifying hosts that are infected by malware is part of every malware incident. Once identified, infected hosts can undergo the appropriate containment, eradication, and recovery actions. Unfortunately, identifying all infected hosts is often complicated by the dynamic nature of computing. For instance, people shut hosts down, disconnect them from networks, or move them from place to place, making it extremely difficult to identify which hosts are currently infected. In addition, some hosts can boot to multiple OSs or use virtual operating system software; an infection in one OS instantiation might not be detectable when a host is currently using another OS.

Accurate identification of infected hosts can also be complicated by other factors. For example, hosts with unmitigated vulnerabilities might be disinfected and reinfected multiple times. Some instances of malware actually remove some or all traces of other malware, which could cause the partially or fully removed infections to go undetected. In addition, the data concerning infected hosts might come from several sources—antivirus software, IDSs, SIEMs, user reports, and other methods—and be very difficult to consolidate and keep current.

Given the number of malware threats, all infection identification should be performed through automated means (as described in Sections 4.2.2.1 and 4.2.2.2). Manual identification methods, such as relying on users to identify and report infected hosts, and having technical staff personally check each host, are not feasible for most situations. Organizations should carefully consider host identification issues so that they are prepared to use multiple identification strategies as part of implementing effective containment strategies. Organizations should also determine which types of identifying information might be needed and what data sources might record the information. For example, a host's current IP address is typically needed for remote actions; of course, a host's physical location is needed for local actions. One piece of information can often be used to determine others, such as mapping an IP address to a media access control (MAC) address, which could then be mapped to a switch serving a particular group of offices. If an IP address can be mapped to a host owner or user—for example, by recording the mapping during network login—the owner or user can be contacted to provide the host's location.

The difficulty in identifying the physical location of an infected host depends on several factors. In a managed environment, identifying a host's location is often relatively easy because of the standardized manner in which things are done. For example, host names might contain the user's ID or office number, or the host's serial number (which can be tied to a user ID). Also, asset inventory management tools might contain current information on host characteristics. In other environments, especially those in which users have full control over their hosts and network management is not centralized, it might be challenging to link a machine to a location. For example, an administrator might know that the host at address 10.3.1.70 appears to be infected but not have any idea where that machine resides or who uses it. Administrators might need to track down an infected host through network devices. For example, a switch port mapper can poll switches for a particular IP address and identify the switch port number and host name associated with that IP address. If the infected host is several switches away, it can take hours to track down a single machine; if the infected host is not directly switched, the administrator might still need to manually trace connectivity through various wiring closets and network devices. An alternative is to pull the network cable or shut down the switch port for an apparently infected host and wait for a user to report an outage. This approach can inadvertently cause a loss of connectivity for small numbers of uninfected hosts, but if performed carefully as a last-resort identification and containment method, it can be quite effective.

Some organizations first make reasonable efforts to identify infected hosts and perform containment, eradication, and recovery efforts on them, then implement measures to prevent hosts that have not been verified as uninfected and properly secured from attaching to the network. These measures should be discussed well in advance, and incident handlers should have prior written permission to lock out hosts under certain circumstances. Generally, lockout measures are based on the characteristics of particular hosts, such as MAC addresses or static IP addresses, but lockouts can also be performed based on user ID if a host is associated with a single user. Another possibility is to use network login scripts to identify and deny access to infected hosts, but this might be ineffective if an infected host starts spreading malware after system boot but before user authentication. As described in Section 4.3.4, having a separate VLAN for infected or unverified hosts can provide a good way to lock out hosts, as long as the mechanism to detect infections is reliable. Although lockout methods might be needed only under extreme circumstances, organizations should think in advance about how individual hosts or users could be locked out so that if needed, lockouts can be performed rapidly.

Sections 4.2.2.1 through 4.2.2.3 discuss the possible categories of infected host identification techniques: forensic, active, and manual.

4.2.2.1. Forensic Identification

Forensic identification is the practice of identifying infected hosts by looking for evidence of recent infections. The evidence may be very recent (only a few minutes old) or not so recent (hours or days old); the older the information is, the less accurate it is likely to be. The most obvious sources of evidence are those that are designed to identify malware activity, such as antivirus software, content filtering (e.g., anti-spam measures), IPS, and SIEM technologies. The logs of security applications might contain detailed records of suspicious activity, and might also indicate whether a security compromise occurred or was prevented.

In situations in which the typical sources of evidence do not contain the necessary information, organizations might need to turn to secondary sources, such as the following:

- **DNS Server Logs.** DNS server logs often contain records of infected hosts attempting to get the IP address for an external malicious site that they are trying to interact with (e.g., send data to, receive commands from). Some organizations deploy passive DNS collection systems, which keep track of all DNS resolutions occurring within the enterprise; these are often more helpful than DNS server logs in identifying malicious activity because malware might use DNS services other than the organization's. Analysts should be cautious of blocking hosts based only on resolved IP addresses because many current attacks use fast flux DNS, which means that each domain resolves to several different IP addresses (in a round robin arrangement), and these addresses often change in a matter of hours. The newer the DNS resolution, the more likely the IP addresses are to be the correct ones to block in the short term.
- **Other Application Server Logs.** Applications commonly used as malware transmission mechanisms, such as email and HTTP, might record information in their logs that indicates which hosts were infected. From end to end, information regarding a single email message might be recorded in several places: the sender's host, each email server that handles the message, and the recipient's host, as well as antivirus and content filtering servers. Similarly, hosts running web browsers can provide a rich resource for information on malicious web activity, including a history of websites visited and the dates and times that they were visited, and cached web data files.

- **Network Forensic Tools.** Software programs that capture and record packets, such as network forensic analysis tools and packet sniffers, might have highly detailed information on malware activity. However, because these tools record so much information about most or all network activity, it can be very time-intensive to extract just the needed information. More efficient means of identifying infected hosts are often available.
- **Network Device Logs.** Firewalls, routers, and other filtering devices that record connection activity, as well as network monitoring tools, might be helpful in identifying network connection activity (e.g., specific port number combinations, unusual protocols) consistent with certain malware.

Using forensic data for identifying infected hosts can be advantageous over other methods because the data has already been collected—the pertinent data just needs to be extracted from the total data set. Unfortunately, for some data sources, extracting the data can take a considerable amount of time. Also, event information can become outdated quickly, causing uninfected hosts to undergo containment unnecessarily and allowing infected hosts to avoid containment measures. If an accurate, comprehensive, and reasonably current source of forensic data is available, it might provide the most effective way of identifying infected hosts.

4.2.2.2. Active Identification

Active identification methods are used to identify which hosts are currently infected. Immediately after identifying an infection, some active approaches can be used to perform containment and eradication measures for the host, such as running a disinfection utility, deploying patches or antivirus updates, or moving the host to a VLAN for infected hosts. Active identification can be performed through several methods, including the following:

- **Security Automation.** Security automation technologies, particularly those used for continuous monitoring (e.g., network access control technologies), can be used to check host characteristics for signs of a current infection, such as a particular configuration setting or a system file with a certain size that indicates an infection. Security automation technologies are generally the preferred method for active identification.

- **Custom Network-Based IPS or IDS Signature.** Writing a custom IPS or IDS signature that identifies infected hosts is often a highly effective technique. Some organizations have separate IPS or IDS sensors with strong signature-writing capabilities that can be dedicated to identifying malware infections. This provides a high-quality source of information while keeping other sensors from becoming overloaded with malware alerts.
- **Packet Sniffers and Protocol Analyzers.** Configuring packet sniffers and protocol analyzers to look only for network traffic matching the characteristics of a particular malware threat can be effective at identifying infected hosts. An example of what to monitor is to look for botnet command and control communications being carried over IRC. These packet examination techniques are most helpful if most or all malware-generated network traffic attempts to pass through the same network device or a few devices.

Although active approaches can produce highly accurate results, active approaches need to be used repeatedly because the status of infections changes constantly and the data is gathered over a period of time.

4.2.2.3. Manual Identification

Another method for identifying infected hosts is the manual approach. This is by far the most labor-intensive of the three methods. It should only be considered in those situations where automated methods are not feasible, such as when networks are completely overwhelmed by infection-related traffic using spoofed addresses. Also, if users have full control over their hosts, as they do in many non-managed environments, the characteristics of hosts may be so different that the results of automated identification methods are quite incomplete and inaccurate. In such situations, a manual approach might be needed to supplement automated approaches.

There are a few possible techniques for implementing a manual approach. One is to ask users to identify infections themselves by providing them with information on the malware and the signs of an infection, as well as antivirus software, OS or application patches, or scanning tools. These items may need to be distributed on removable media. A similar manual technique is to have local IT staffers (including individuals who normally do not participate in malware incident handling) either check all hosts or check hosts that are suspected of being infected. In some cases, non-IT staff might fulfill this duty at remote offices that do not have available IT staff. Any staff who might need to assist during major malware incidents should be designated in advance and provided with documentation and periodic training on their possible duties.

4.2.2.4. Identification Recommendations

Although active approaches typically produce the most accurate results, they are often not the fastest way of identifying infections. It might take considerable time to scan every host in an organization, and because hosts that have been disconnected or shut off will not be identified, the scan will need to be repeated. If forensic data is very recent, it might be a good source of readily available information, although the information might not be comprehensive. Manual methods are generally not feasible for comprehensive enterprise-wide identification, but they are a necessary part of identification when other methods are not sufficient. In many cases, it is most effective to use multiple approaches simultaneously or in sequence to provide the best results.

Organizations should carefully consider the possible approaches for their environment ahead of time, select a sufficiently broad range of approaches, and develop procedures and technical capabilities to perform each selected approach effectively when a malware incident occurs. Organizations should also identify which individuals or groups can assist in identification efforts. For example, identification might be performed by security administrators, system administrators, network administrators, desktop administrators, mobile device administrators, and others, depending on the sources of identification information. Organizations should ensure that everyone who might be involved in identification knows what his or her role is and how to perform necessary tasks.

4.2.3. Prioritizing Incident Response

Once a malware incident has been validated, the next activity is to prioritize its handling. NIST SP 800-61 presents general guidelines for incident prioritization; this section extends those by including additional factors to consider during prioritization.

Certain forms of malware, such as worms, tend to spread very quickly and can cause a substantial impact in minutes or hours, so they often necessitate a high-priority response. Other forms of malware, such as Trojan horses, tend to affect a single host; the response to such incidents should be based on the value of the data and services provided by the host. Organizations should establish a set of criteria that identify the appropriate level of response for various malware-related situations. The criteria should incorporate considerations such as the following:

- How the malware entered the environment and what transmission mechanisms it uses
- What type of malware it is (e.g., virus, worm, Trojan horse)
- Which types of attacker tools are placed onto the host by the malware
- What networks and hosts the malware is affecting and how it is affecting them
- How the impact of the incident is likely to increase in the following minutes, hours, and days if the incident is not contained.

4.2.4. Malware Analysis

Incident handlers can study the behavior of malware by analyzing it either actively (executing the malware) or forensically (examining the infected host for evidence of malware). Forensic approaches are safer to perform on an infected host because they can examine the host without allowing the malware to continue executing. However, sometimes it is significantly faster and easier to analyze malware by monitoring it during execution. Such active approaches are best performed on malware test systems instead of production hosts, to minimize possible damage caused by allowing the malware to execute.

Ideal active approaches involve an incident handler acquiring a malware sample from an infected host and placing the malware on an isolated test system. Test systems often have a virtualized OS image; copies of these builds can be infected, isolating any infection within the virtualized OS, and the infected image can be replaced with a known good image after the analysis is complete.[17] On such test systems, the host OS is kept uninfected so it can be used to monitor the execution of the malware within the virtualized OS. The test system should include up-to-date tools for identifying malware (e.g., antivirus software, intrusion detection systems), listing the currently running processes, and displaying network connections, as well as many other potentially helpful utilities. There are various websites and books that provide detailed instructions on setting up malware test systems and their tools; further discussion of them is outside the scope of this publication. Malware test systems are helpful not only for analyzing current malware threats without the risk of inadvertently causing additional damage to the organization, but also for training staff in malware incident handling.

Forensic approaches involve booting a forensic environment and using it to study the stored information from an infected host. The toolsets for forensic analysis greatly overlap those for active analysis; similarly, there are various websites and books available that explain how to create forensic analysis environments. There are two basic approaches: create a bootable forensic environment on write-protected removable media, or use a forensic workstation and connect it to the storage of the infected host (e.g., hard drive). The motivation for using such a trusted toolkit instead of relying on the information reported by the infected host's OS is that malware on the host may have disabled or altered the functionality of the security tools on the infected host, such as antivirus software, so that they do not report malicious activity. By running tools from a protected, verified toolkit, incident handlers can gain a more accurate understanding of the activity on the host.

4.3. Containment

Containment of malware has two major components: stopping the spread of the malware and preventing further damage to hosts. Nearly every malware incident requires containment actions. In addressing an incident, it is important for an organization to decide which methods of containment to employ initially, early in the response. Containment of isolated incidents and incidents involving noninfectious forms of malware is generally straightforward, involving such actions as disconnecting the affected hosts from networks or shutting down the hosts. For more widespread malware incidents, such as fast-spreading worms, organizations should use a strategy that contains the incident for most hosts as quickly as possible; this should limit the number of machines that are infected, the amount of damage that is done, and the amount of time that it will take to fully recover all data and services.

In containing a malware incident, it is also important to understand that stopping the spread of malware does not necessarily prevent further damage to hosts. Malware on a host might continue to exfiltrate sensitive data, replace OS files, or cause other damage. In addition, some instances of malware are designed to cause additional damage when network connectivity is lost or other containment measures are performed. For example, an infected host might run a malicious process that contacts another host periodically. If that connectivity is lost because the infected host is disconnected from the network, the malware might overwrite all the data on the host's hard drive. For these reasons, handlers should not assume that just because a host has been disconnected from the network, further damage to the host has been prevented, and in many cases, should begin eradication efforts as soon as possible to prevent more damage.

Organizations should have strategies and procedures in place for making containment-related decisions that reflect the level of risk acceptable to the organization. For example, an organization might decide that infected hosts performing critical functions should not be disconnected from networks or shut down if the likely damage to the organization from those functions being unavailable would be greater than the security risks posed by not isolating or shutting down the host. Containment strategies should support incident handlers in selecting the appropriate combination of containment methods based on the characteristics of a particular situation.

Containment methods can be divided into four basic categories: relying on user participation, performing automated detection, temporarily halting services, and blocking certain types of network connectivity. Sections 4.3.1 through 4.3.4 describe each category in detail.

4.3.1. Containment Through User Participation

At one time, user participation was a valuable part of containment efforts, particularly during large-scale incidents in non-managed environments. Users were provided with instructions on how to identify infections and what measures to take if a host was infected, such as calling the help desk, disconnecting the host from the network, or powering off the host. The instructions might also cover malware eradication, such as updating antivirus signatures and performing a host scan, or obtaining and running a specialized malware eradication utility. As hosts have increasingly become managed, user participation in containment has sharply decreased. However, having users perform containment actions is still helpful in non-managed environments and other situations in which use of fully automated containment methods (such as those described in Sections 4.3.2 through 4.3.4) is not feasible.

Effectively communicating helpful information to users in a timely manner is challenging. Although email is typically the most efficient communication mechanism, it might be unavailable during certain incidents, or users might not read the email until it is too late. Therefore, organizations should have several alternate mechanisms in place for distributing information to users, such as sending messages to all voice mailboxes within the organization, posting signs in work areas, and handing out instructions at building and office entrances. Organizations with significant numbers of users in alternate locations, such as home offices and small branch offices, should ensure that the communication mechanisms reach these users. Another important consideration is that users might need to be provided with software, such as cleanup utilities, and software updates, such as patches and updated antivirus signatures. Organizations should identify and implement multiple methods for delivering software utilities and updates to users who are expected to assist with containment.

Although user participation can be very helpful for containment, organizations should not rely on this means for containing malware incidents unless absolutely necessary. No matter how containment guidance is communicated, it is unlikely that all users will receive it and realize that it might pertain to them. In addition, some users who receive containment instructions are unlikely to follow the directions successfully because of a lack of understanding, a mistake in following the directions, or host-specific characteristics or variations in the malware that make the directions incorrect for that host. Some users also might be focused on performing their regular tasks and be unconcerned about the possible effects of malware on their hosts. Nevertheless, for large-scale incidents involving a sizable percentage of the organization's hosts in non-managed environments, user involvement in containment can significantly reduce the burden on incident handlers and technical support staff in responding to the incident.

4.3.2. Containment Through Automated Detection

Many malware incidents can be contained primarily through the use of the automated technologies described in Section 3.4 for preventing and detecting infections. These technologies include antivirus software, content filtering, and intrusion prevention software. Because antivirus software on hosts can detect and remove infections, it is often the preferred automated detection method for assisting in containment. However, as previously discussed, many of today's malware threats are novel, so antivirus software and other technologies often fail to recognize them as being malicious. Also, malware that compromises the OS may disable security controls such as antivirus software, particularly in unmanaged environments where users have greater control over their hosts. Containment through antivirus software is not as robust and effective as it used to be.

Organizations should be prepared to use other security tools to contain the malware until the antivirus signatures can perform the containment effectively, if antivirus signatures become available at all.[18] After an organization receives updated signatures, it is prudent to test them at least minimally before deployment, to ensure that the update itself should not cause a negative impact on the organization. Another benefit of having multiple types of automated detection ready is that different detectors may be more effective in different situations. For example, detection tools that were not capable of recognizing or stopping malware when it was a new threat can sometimes be updated or reconfigured to recognize the same malware's characteristics later and stop it from spreading. Examples of automated detection methods other than antivirus software are as follows:

- **Content Filtering.** For example, email servers and clients, as well as anti-spam software, can be configured to block emails or email attachments that have certain characteristics, such as a known bad subject, sender, message text, or attachment name or type.[19] This is only helpful when the malware has static characteristics; highly customized malware usually cannot be blocked effectively using content filtering. Web content filtering and other content filtering technologies may also be of use for static malware.
- **Network-Based IPS Software.** Most IPS products allow their prevention capabilities to be enabled for specific signatures. If a network-based IPS device is inline, meaning that it is an active part of the network, and it has a signature for the malware, it should be able to identify the malware and stop it from reaching its targets. If the IPS device does not have its prevention capabilities enabled, it may be prudent during a severe incident to reconfigure or redeploy one or more IPS sensors and enable IPS so they can stop the activity. IPS technologies should be able to stop both incoming and outgoing infection attempts. Of course, the value of IPSs in malware containment depends on the availability and accuracy of a signature to identify the malware. Several IPS products allow administrators to write custom signatures based on some of the known characteristics of the malware, or to customize existing signatures. For example, an IPS may allow administrators to specify known bad email attachment names or subjects, or to specify known bad destination port numbers. In many cases, IPS administrators can have their own accurate signature in place hours before antivirus vendors have signatures available. In addition, because the IPS signature affects only network-based IPS sensors, whereas antivirus signatures generally affect all workstations and servers, it is generally less risky to rapidly deploy a new IPS signature than new antivirus signatures.
- **Executable Blacklisting.** Some operating systems, host-based IPS products, and other technologies can restrict certain executables from being run. For example, administrators can enter the names of files that should not be executed. If antivirus signatures are not yet available for a new threat, it might be possible to configure a

blacklisting technology to block the execution of the files that are part of the new threat.

4.3.3. Containment Through Disabling Services

Some malware incidents necessitate more drastic and potentially disruptive measures for containment. These incidents make extensive use of a particular service. Containing such an incident quickly and effectively might be accomplished through a loss of services, such as shutting down a service used by malware, blocking a certain service at the network perimeter, or disabling portions of a service (e.g., large mailing lists). Also, a service might provide a channel for infection or for transferring data from infected hosts—for example, a botnet command and control channel using Internet Relay Chat (IRC). In either case, shutting down the affected services might be the best way to contain the infection without losing all services. This action is typically performed at the application level (e.g., disabling a service on servers) or at the network level (e.g., configuring firewalls to block IP addresses or ports associated with a service). The goal is to disable as little functionality as possible while containing the incident effectively. To support the disabling of network services, organizations should maintain lists of the services they use and the TCP and UDP ports used by each service.

From a technology standpoint, disabling a service is generally a simple process; understanding the consequences of doing so tends to be more challenging. Disabling a service that the organization relies on has an obvious negative impact on the organization's functions. Also, disabling a service might inadvertently disrupt other services that depend on it. For example, disabling email services could impair directory services that replicate information through email. Organizations should maintain a list of dependencies between major services so that incident handlers are aware of them when making containment decisions. Also, organizations might find it helpful to provide alternative services with similar functionality. For example, in a highly managed environment, if a vulnerability in an email client were being exploited by a new virus, users could be blocked temporarily from using that email client and instead directed to use a web-based email client that did not have the vulnerability. This step would help contain the incident while providing users with email access. The same strategy could be used for cases involving exploitation of vulnerabilities in web browsers and other common client applications.

4.3.4. Containment Through Disabling Connectivity

Containing incidents by placing temporary restrictions on network connectivity can be very effective. For example, if infected hosts attempt to establish connections with an external host to download rootkits, handlers should consider blocking all access to the external host (by IP address or domain name, as appropriate). Similarly, if infected hosts within the organization attempt to spread their malware, the organization might block network traffic from the hosts' IP addresses to control the situation while the infected hosts are physically located and disinfected. An alternative to blocking network access for particular IP addresses is to disconnect the infected hosts from the network, which could be accomplished by reconfiguring network devices to deny network access or physically disconnecting network cables from infected hosts.

The most drastic containment step is purposely breaking needed network connectivity for uninfected hosts. This could eliminate network access for groups of hosts, such as remote VPN users. In worst-case scenarios, isolating subnets from the primary network or the Internet might be necessary to stop the spread of malware, halt damage to hosts, and provide an opportunity to mitigate vulnerabilities. Implementing a widespread loss of connectivity to achieve containment is most likely to be acceptable to an organization in cases in which malware activity is already causing severe network disruptions or infected hosts are performing an attack against other organizations. Because a major loss of connectivity almost always affects many organizational functions, connectivity usually must be restored as soon as possible.

Organizations can design and implement their networks to make containment through loss of connectivity easier to do and less disruptive. For example, some organizations place their servers and workstations on separate subnets; during a malware incident targeting workstations, the infected workstation subnets can be isolated from the main network, and the server subnets can continue to provide functionality to external customers and internal workstation subnets that are not infected. Another network design strategy related to malware containment is the use of separate virtual local area networks (VLAN) for infected hosts. With this design, a host's security posture is checked when it wants to join the network, and also may be checked periodically while connected. The security checking is often done through network access control software by placing on each host an agent that monitors various characteristics of the host, such as OS patches and antivirus updates. When the host attempts to connect to the network, a network device such as a router requests information from the host's agent. If the host does not respond to the request or the response indicates that the host is insecure, the network device causes the host to be placed onto a separate VLAN. The same technique can be used with hosts that are already on the organization's regular networks, allowing infected hosts to be moved automatically to a separate VLAN.

Having a separate VLAN for infected hosts also helps organizations to provide antivirus signature updates and OS and application patches to the hosts while severely restricting what they can do. Without a separate VLAN, the organization might need to remove infected hosts' network access entirely, which necessitates transferring and applying updates manually to each host to contain and eradicate the malware and mitigate vulnerabilities. A variant of the separate VLAN strategy that can be effective in some situations is to place all hosts on a particular network segment in a VLAN and then move hosts to the production network as each is deemed to be clean and remediated.

4.3.5. Containment Recommendations

Containment can be performed through many methods in the four categories described above (users, automated detection, loss of services, and loss of connectivity). Because no single malware containment category or individual method is appropriate or effective in every situation, incident handlers should select a combination of containment methods that is likely to be effective in containing the current incident while limiting damage to hosts and reducing the impact that containment methods might have on other hosts. For example, shutting down all network access might be very effective at stopping the spread of malware, but it would also allow infections on hosts to continue damaging files and would disrupt many important functions of the organization.

The most drastic containment methods can be tolerated by most organizations for only a brief period of time. Accordingly, organizations should support sound containment decisions by having policies that clearly state who has authority to make major containment decisions and under what circumstances various actions (e.g., disconnecting subnets from the Internet) are appropriate.

4.4. Eradication

Although the primary goal of eradication is to remove malware from infected hosts, eradication is typically more involved than that. If an infection was successful because of a host vulnerability or other security weakness, such as an unsecured file share, then eradication includes the elimination or mitigation of that weakness, which should prevent the host from becoming reinfected or becoming infected by another instance of malware or a variant of the original threat. Eradication actions are often consolidated with containment efforts. For example, organizations might run a utility that identifies infected hosts, applies patches to remove vulnerabilities, and runs antivirus software that removes infections. Containment actions often limit eradication choices; for example, if an incident is contained by disconnecting infected hosts from the primary network, the hosts should either be connected to a separate VLAN so that they can be updated remotely, or patched and reconfigured manually. Because the hosts are disconnected from the primary network, the incident handlers will be under pressure to perform eradication actions on the hosts as quickly as possible so that the users can regain full use of their hosts.

Different situations necessitate various combinations of eradication techniques. In cases where disinfection is possible, the most common tools for eradication are antivirus software, vulnerability management technologies, network access control software, and other tools designed to remove malware and correct vulnerabilities. Automated eradication methods, such as triggering antivirus scans remotely, are much more efficient than manual methods, such as visiting infected hosts in person and running disinfection software from a CD. As described in Section 4.3.1, some situations necessitate user participation in containment and eradication activities. Providing instructions and software updates to users works in some cases, but other users might need assistance. Having formal or informal walk-up help desk areas at major facilities can also be effective and is more efficient and convenient than having IT staff locate and interrupt each affected user. During major incidents, additional IT staff members can be relieved of other duties temporarily to assist in eradication efforts. For locations without IT staff, it is often helpful to have a few people trained in basic eradication actions so that they can take care of their own hosts. Organizations should be prepared to perform a few different types of eradication efforts simultaneously if needed.

For many malware incidents, simple disinfection is not feasible, so it is necessary to rebuild all infected hosts as part of eradication efforts. Rebuilding includes the reinstallation and securing of the OS and applications (or restoration of known good OS and application backups, including the use of built-in OS rollback capabilities), and the restoration of data from known good backups. Some types of malware are extremely difficult to remove from hosts; even if they can be removed, each host's OS may be damaged, possibly to the point where the hosts cannot boot. Rebuilding is also the best eradication option when the actions performed on an infected host are unknown. If a host has multiple infections; has been infected for an extended or unknown period of time; or has had backdoors, rootkits, or other damaging attacker tools installed, other malicious actions besides the malware infections may have been performed against the host. In such cases, rebuilding the host would be the most reliable way of restoring its integrity. Also, in some cases it is faster to rebuild a host than to perform all of the analysis necessary to determine exactly what the malware has done and remove all traces of it from the host. This is particularly true in managed environments where hosts are built based on standard OS images, baselines, etc. Organizations should be prepared to rebuild hosts quickly, as needed, when malware incidents occur.

In general, organizations should rebuild any host that has any of the following incident characteristics, instead of performing typical eradication actions (disinfection):

- One or more attackers gained administrator-level access to the host.
- Unauthorized administrator-level access to the host was available to anyone through a backdoor, an unprotected share created by a worm, or other means.
- System files were replaced by a Trojan horse, backdoor, rootkit, attacker tools, or other means.
- The host is unstable or does not function properly after the malware has been eradicated by antivirus software or other programs or techniques. This indicates that either the malware has not been eradicated completely or that it has caused damage to important system or application files or settings.
- There is doubt about the nature of and extent of the infection or any unauthorized access gained because of the infection.

If a malware incident does not have any of these characteristics, then it is typically sufficient to eradicate the malware from the host instead of rebuilding the host.

Eradication can be frustrating because of the number of hosts to clean up and the tendency to have additional infections and reinfections occurring for days, weeks, or months.[20] Incident handlers should periodically perform identification activities to identify hosts that are still infected and estimate the success of the eradication. A reduction in the number of infected hosts would demonstrate that the incident response team was making progress and would help the team choose the best strategy for handling the remaining hosts and allocate sufficient time and resources. It can be tempting to declare an incident resolved once the number of infected hosts has dropped significantly from the original numbers, but the organization should strive to reduce the suspected numbers of infected and vulnerable machines to low enough levels that if they were all connected to the network at once and the vulnerable machines all became infected, the overall impact of the infections would be minimal.

4.5. Recovery

The two main aspects of recovery from malware incidents are restoring the functionality and data of infected hosts and removing temporary containment measures. Additional actions to restore hosts are not necessary for most malware incidents that cause limited host damage (for example, an infection that simply altered a few data files and was completely removable with antivirus software). As discussed in Section 4.4, for malware incidents that are far more damaging, such as Trojan horses, rootkits, or backdoors, corrupting thousands of system and data files, or wiping out hard drives, it is often best to first rebuild the host, then secure the host so that it is no longer vulnerable to the malware threat. Organizations should carefully consider possible worst-case scenarios, such as a new malware threat that necessitates rebuilding a large percentage of the organization's workstations, and determine how the hosts would be recovered in these cases. This should include identifying who would perform the recovery tasks, estimating how many hours of labor would be needed and how much calendar time would elapse, and determining how the recovery efforts should be prioritized.

Determining when to remove temporary containment measures, such as suspended services (e.g., email) or connectivity (e.g., Internet access, VPN for telecommuters), is often a difficult decision during major malware incidents. For example, suppose that email has been shut down to stop the spread of a malware infection while vulnerable hosts are patched and infected hosts undergo individual malware containment, eradication, and recovery measures. It might take days or weeks for all vulnerable hosts to be located and patched and for all infected hosts to be cleaned, but email cannot remain suspended for that period of time. When email service is restored, it is almost certain that an infected host will begin spreading the malware again at some time. However, if nearly all hosts have been patched and cleaned, the impact of a new malware infection should be minimal. Incident response teams should strive to keep containment measures in place until the estimated number of infected hosts and hosts vulnerable to infection is sufficiently low that subsequent incidents should be of little consequence. Incident handlers should also consider alternative containment measures that could adequately maintain containment of the incident while causing less of an impact on the normal functions of the organization. However, even though the incident response team should assess the risks of restoring the service, management should ultimately be responsible for determining what should be done, based on the incident response team's recommendations and management's understanding of the business impact of maintaining the containment measures.

4.6. Lessons Learned

When a major malware incident occurs, the primary individuals performing the response usually work intensively for days or weeks. As the major handling efforts end, the key people are usually mentally and physically fatigued, and are behind in performing other tasks that were pending during the incident handling period. Consequently, the lessons learned phase of incident response might be significantly delayed or skipped altogether for major malware incidents. However, because major malware incidents can be extremely expensive to handle, it is particularly important for organizations to conduct robust lessons learned activities for major malware incidents. Although it is reasonable to give handlers and other key people a few days to catch up on other tasks, review meetings and other efforts should occur expeditiously, while the incident is still fresh in everyone's minds. The lessons learned process for malware incidents is no different than for any other type of incident. Examples of possible outcomes of lessons learned activities for malware incidents are as follows:

- **Security Policy Changes.** Security policies might be modified to prevent similar incidents. For example, if connecting personally owned mobile devices to organization laptops caused a serious infection, modifying the organization's policies to secure, restrict, or prohibit such device connections might be advisable.
- **Awareness Program Changes.** Security awareness training for users might be changed to reduce the number of infections or to improve users' actions in reporting incidents and assisting with handling incidents on their own hosts.

- **Software Reconfiguration.** OS or application settings might need to be changed to support security policy changes or to achieve compliance with existing policy.
- **Malware Detection Software Deployment.** If hosts were infected through a transmission mechanism that was unprotected by antivirus software or other malware detection tools, an incident might provide sufficient justification to purchase and deploy additional software.
- **Malware Detection Software Reconfiguration.** Detection software might need to be reconfigured in various ways, such as the following:
  - Increasing the frequency of software and signature updates
  - Improving the accuracy of detection (e.g., fewer false positives, fewer false negatives)
  - Increasing the scope of monitoring (e.g., monitoring additional transmission mechanisms, monitoring additional files or file systems)
  - Changing the action automatically performed in response to detected malware
  - Improving the efficiency of update distribution.

APPENDIX A—GLOSSARY

Selected terms used in the guide are defined below.

Antivirus Software: A program that monitors a computer or network to identify all major types of malware and prevent or contain malware incidents.

Backdoor: A malicious program that listens for commands on a certain Transmission Control Protocol (TCP) or User Datagram Protocol (UDP) port.

Disinfecting: Removing malware from within a file.

False Negative: An instance in which a security tool intended to detect a particular threat fails to do so.

False Positive: An instance in which a security tool incorrectly classifies benign content as malicious.

Malware: A program that is covertly inserted into another program with the intent to destroy data, run destructive or intrusive programs, or otherwise compromise the confidentiality, integrity, or availability of the victim's data, applications, or operating system.

Mobile Code: Software that is transmitted from a remote host to be executed on a local host, typically without the user's explicit instruction.

On-Access Scanning: Configuring a security tool to perform real-time scans of each file for malware as the file is downloaded, opened, or executed.

On-Demand Scanning: Allowing users to launch security tool scans for malware on a computer as desired.

Phishing: Tricking individuals into disclosing sensitive personal information through deceptive computer-based means.

Quarantining: Storing files containing malware in isolation for future disinfection or examination.

Rootkit: A collection of files that is installed on a host to alter the standard functionality of the host in a malicious and stealthy way.

Signature: A set of characteristics of known malware instances that can be used to identify known malware and some new variants of known malware.

APPENDIX B—ACRONYMS AND ABBREVIATIONS

Selected acronyms and abbreviations used in the guide are defined below.

ACL	Access Control List
CSRC	Computer Security Resource Center
DDoS	Distributed Denial of Service
DMARC	Domain-based Message Authentication, Reporting & Conformance
DNS	Domain Name System
FAQ	Frequently Asked Questions
FISMA	Federal Information Security Management Act
HTML	Hypertext Markup Language
HTTP	Hypertext Transfer Protocol
ICMP	Internet Control Message Protocol
ID	Identification
IDS	Intrusion Detection System
IETF	Internet Engineering Task Force
IP	Internet Protocol
IPS	Intrusion Prevention System
IT	Information Technology
ITL	Information Technology Laboratory
MAC	Media Access Control
NAP	Network Access Protection
NAT	Network Address Translation

NIST National Institute of Standards and Technology
NSRL National Software Reference Library
OMB Office of Management and Budget
OS Operating System
PIN Personal Identification Number
RFC Request for Comment
SIEM Security Information and Event Management
SMTP Simple Mail Transfer Protocol
SP Special Publication
TCP Transmission Control Protocol
UDP User Datagram Protocol
USB Universal Serial Bus
US-CERT United States Computer Emergency Readiness Team
VBScript Visual Basic Script
VLAN Virtual Local Area Network
VPN Virtual Private Network

APPENDIX C—RESOURCES

The following lists provide examples of resources that may be helpful in understanding malware and in preventing and handling malware incidents.

Organizations

Organization	URL
Anti-Phishing Working Group (APWG)	http://www.antiphishing.org/
Anti-Virus Information Exchange Network (AVIEN)	http://www.avien.org/
Computer Antivirus Research Organization (CARO)	http://www.caro.org/
Cooperative Association for Internet Data Analysis (CAIDA)	http://www.caida.org/
European Institute for Computer Antivirus Research (EICAR)	http://www.eicar.org/
Internet Storm Center (ISC)	http://isc.incidents.org/
Securelist	http://www.securelist.com/en/
United States Computer Emergency Readiness Team (US-CERT)	http://www.us-cert.gov/
Virus Bulletin	http://www.virusbtn.com/
WildList Organization International	http://www.wildlist.org/

Other Technical Resource Documents

Resource Name	URL
FTC, *How Not to Get Hooked by a "Phishing" Scam*	http://ftc.gov/bcp/conline/pubs/alerts/phishingalrt.htm
IETF, RFC 2267, *Network Ingress Filtering: Defeating Denial of Service Attacks Which Employ IP Source Address Spoofing*	http://www.ietf.org/rfc/rfc2267.txt
NIST, SP 800-28 Version 2, *Guidelines on Active Content and Mobile Code*	http://csrc.nist.gov/publications/PubsSPs.html#800-28
NIST, SP 800-37 Revision 1, *Guide for Applying the Risk Management Framework to Federal Information Systems*	http://csrc.nist.gov/publications/PubsSPs.html#800-37
NIST, SP 800-40 Revision 3, *Guide to Enterprise Patch Management Technologies*	http://csrc.nist.gov/publications/PubsSPs.html#800-40-rev3
NIST, SP 800-41 Revision 1, *Guidelines on Firewalls and Firewall Policy*	http://csrc.nist.gov/publications/PubsSPs.html#800-41
NIST, SP 800-45 Version 2, *Guidelines on Electronic Mail Security*	http://csrc.nist.gov/publications/PubsSPs.html#800-45
NIST, SP 800-53 Revision 3, *Recommended Security Controls for Federal Information Systems and Organizations*	http://csrc.nist.gov/publications/PubsSPs.html#800-53
NIST, SP 800-61 Revision 2, *Computer Security Incident Handling Guide*	http://csrc.nist.gov/publications/PubsSPs.html#800-61-rev2
NIST, SP 800-70 Revision 2, *Security Configuration Checklists Program for IT Products*	http://csrc.nist.gov/checklists/
NIST, SP 800-86, *Guide to Applying Forensic Techniques to Incident Response*	http://csrc.nist.gov/publications/PubsSPs.html#800-86
NIST, SP 800-92, *Guide to Computer Security Log Management*	http://csrc.nist.gov/publications/PubsSPs.html#800-92
NIST, SP 800-94, *Guide to Intrusion Detection and Prevention Systems (IDPS)*	http://csrc.nist.gov/publications/PubsSPs.html#800-94
NIST, SP 800-115, *Technical Guide to Information Security Testing and Assessment*	http://csrc.nist.gov/publications/PubsSPs.html#800-115
NIST, SP 800-117, *Guide to Adopting and Using the Security Content Automation Protocol (SCAP)*	http://csrc.nist.gov/publications/PubsSPs.html#800-117

(Continued)

Resource Name	URL
NIST, SP 800-128, *Guide for Security-Focused Configuration Management of Information Systems*	http://csrc.nist.gov/publications/PubsSPs.html#800-128

End Notes

[1] http://csrc.nist.gov/publications/PubsSPs.html#800-37

[2] http://csrc.nist.gov/publications/PubsSPs.html#800-61-rev2

[3] For more information on phishing, including examples of recent phishing attacks, visit the Anti-Phishing Working Group website (http://www.antiphishing.org/). Another good resource is *How Not to Get Hooked by a "Phishing" Scam*, from the Federal Trade Commission (FTC) (http://www.ftc.gov/bcp/edu/pubs/consumer/alerts/alt127.shtm).

[4] See NIST SP 800-61 for more information on this type of information sharing (e.g., blogs and data feeds from antimalware product vendors, incident response organizations, Information Sharing and Analysis Centers)

[5] For example, many acceptable use policies state that the organization's computing resources should be used only in support of the organization. Personal use of computing resources is a common source of malware incidents; however, because there are several other reasons why an organization might want to restrict personal use of computing resources, this policy consideration is more appropriately addressed in the organization's acceptable use policy than a malware policy.

[6] Although all of these considerations are intended to help organizations prevent malware incidents, many of them could also be helpful in detecting or containing incidents.

[7] For more information, see NIST SP 800-128, *Guide for Security-Focused Configuration Management of Information Systems* (http://csrc.nist.gov/publications/PubsSPs.html#800-128).

[8] For more information on security automation and checklists, see NIST SP 800-70 Revision 2, *National Checklist Program for IT Products: Guidelines for Checklist Users and Developers* (http://csrc.nist.gov/publications/PubsSPs.html#800-70) and NIST SP 800-117, *Guide to Adopting and Using the Security Content Automation Protocol (SCAP)* (http://csrc.nist.gov/publications/PubsSPs.html#800-117). More information on patch management is available from NIST SP 800-40 Revision 3, *Guide to Enterprise Patch Management Technologies* (http://csrc.nist.gov/publications/PubsSPs.html#800-40-rev3).

[9] Intrusion prevention systems are similar to intrusion detection systems (IDS), except that IPSs can attempt to stop malicious activity, whereas IDSs cannot. This section discusses the use of IPSs, not IDSs, for preventing or containing malware incidents. Section 4 describes how both IPS and IDS technologies can be used for malware incident detection.

[10] http://csrc.nist.gov/publications/PubsSPs.html#800-94

[11] The use of some services cannot be blocked easily through firewall rulesets. For example, some peer-to-peer file sharing services and instant messaging services can use port numbers designated for other services, such as HTTP or Simple Mail Transfer Protocol (SMTP). Attempting to prevent the use of such services by blocking port numbers might cause

legitimate services to be blocked. In such cases, it might be necessary to block access to particular IP addresses that host portions of the services, such as instant messaging servers. Also, as described later in this section, application proxies can identify some instances in which one service is used when another is expected.

[12] In addition to the standard spam filtering technologies, there are also emerging solutions that aim to reduce spam through email authentication. An example is the Domain-based Message Authentication, Reporting & Conformance (DMARC) specification (http://www.dmarc.org/).

[13] This paragraph was taken from the Executive Summary of NIST SP 800-147, *BIOS Protection Guidelines*.

[14] http://csrc.nist.gov/publications/PubsSPs.html#800-147

[15] For more information on virtualization, see NIST SP 800-125, *Guide to Security for Full Virtualization Technologies* (http://csrc.nist.gov/publications/PubsSPs.html#800-125).

[16] For more information on how to establish an incident response capability, refer to NIST SP 800-61, *Computer Security Incident Handling Guide*, available at http://csrc.nist.gov/publications/PubsSPs.html#800-61.

[17] Some malware can detect the presence of a virtualized environment and change their behavior accordingly.

[18] Incident handlers should also be familiar with the organization's policy and procedures for submitting copies of unknown malware to the organization's antivirus vendors and other security software vendors for analysis. This practice can help vendors respond more quickly to new threats. Organizations should also contact trusted parties, such as incident response organizations, when needed for guidance on handling new threats.

[19] Generally, it is feasible only in highly managed environments to configure email clients throughout the organization to block certain emails or email attachments.

[20] Instances of a particular type of malware might reside within an organization indefinitely, regardless of eradication efforts. For example, malware might be captured in host backups; restoration of a backup could also restore the malware. Also, malware might infect removable media that then sits unused for an extended period of time. Years after the initial infection, the removable media could be accessed, and the malware could attempt to infect the host.

In: Malware and Computer Security Incidents ISBN: 978-1-62948-191-3
Editor: Mark Borrelli

Chapter 2

COMPUTER SECURITY INCIDENT HANDLING GUIDE*

Paul Cichonski, Tom Millar, Tim Grance and Karen Scarfone

ABSTRACT

Computer security incident response has become an important component of information technology (IT) programs. Because performing incident response effectively is a complex undertaking, establishing a successful incident response capability requires substantial planning and resources. This publication assists organizations in establishing computer security incident response capabilities and handling incidents efficiently and effectively. This publication provides guidelines for incident handling, particularly for analyzing incident-related data and determining the appropriate response to each incident. The guidelines can be followed independently of particular hardware platforms, operating systems, protocols, or applications.

* This is an edited, reformatted and augmented version of National Institute of Standards and Technology, NIST Special Publication 800-61 Revision 2, dated August 2012.

EXECUTIVE SUMMARY

Computer security incident response has become an important component of information technology (IT) programs. Cybersecurity-related attacks have become not only more numerous and diverse but also more damaging and disruptive. New types of security-related incidents emerge frequently. Preventive activities based on the results of risk assessments can lower the number of incidents, but not all incidents can be prevented. An incident response capability is therefore necessary for rapidly detecting incidents, minimizing loss and destruction, mitigating the weaknesses that were exploited, and restoring IT services. To that end, this publication provides guidelines for incident handling, particularly for analyzing incident-related data and determining the appropriate response to each incident. The guidelines can be followed independently of particular hardware platforms, operating systems, protocols, or applications.

Because performing incident response effectively is a complex undertaking, establishing a successful incident response capability requires substantial planning and resources. Continually monitoring for attacks is essential. Establishing clear procedures for prioritizing the handling of incidents is critical, as is implementing effective methods of collecting, analyzing, and reporting data. It is also vital to build relationships and establish suitable means of communication with other internal groups (e.g., human resources, legal) and with external groups (e.g., other incident response teams, law enforcement).

This publication assists organizations in establishing computer security incident response capabilities and handling incidents efficiently and effectively. This revision of the publication, Revision 2, updates material throughout the publication to reflect the changes in attacks and incidents. Understanding threats and identifying modern attacks in their early stages is key to preventing subsequent compromises, and proactively sharing information among organizations regarding the signs of these attacks is an increasingly effective way to identify them.

Implementing the following requirements and recommendations should facilitate efficient and effective incident response for Federal departments and agencies.

Organizations must create, provision, and operate a formal incident response capability. Federal law requires Federal agencies to report incidents to the United States Computer Emergency Readiness Team (US-CERT) office within the Department of Homeland Security (DHS).

The Federal Information Security Management Act (FISMA) requires Federal agencies to establish incident response capabilities. Each Federal civilian agency must designate a primary and secondary point of contact (POC) with US-CERT and report all incidents consistent with the agency's incident response policy. Each agency is responsible for determining how to fulfill these requirements.

Establishing an incident response capability should include the following actions:

- Creating an incident response policy and plan
- Developing procedures for performing incident handling and reporting
- Setting guidelines for communicating with outside parties regarding incidents
- Selecting a team structure and staffing model
- Establishing relationships and lines of communication between the incident response team and other groups, both internal (e.g., legal department) and external (e.g., law enforcement agencies)
- Determining what services the incident response team should provide
- Staffing and training the incident response team.

Organizations should reduce the frequency of incidents by effectively securing networks, systems, and applications.

Preventing problems is often less costly and more effective than reacting to them after they occur. Thus, incident prevention is an important complement to an incident response capability. If security controls are insufficient, high volumes of incidents may occur. This could overwhelm the resources and capacity for response, which would result in delayed or incomplete recovery and possibly more extensive damage and longer periods of service and data unavailability. Incident handling can be performed more effectively if organizations complement their incident response capability with adequate resources to actively maintain the security of networks, systems, and applications. This includes training IT staff on complying with the organization's security standards and making users aware of policies and procedures regarding appropriate use of networks, systems, and applications.

Organizations should document their guidelines for interactions with other organizations regarding incidents.

During incident handling, the organization will need to communicate with outside parties, such as other incident response teams, law enforcement, the media, vendors, and victim organizations. Because these communications often need to occur quickly, organizations should predetermine communication guidelines so that only the appropriate information is shared with the right parties.

Organizations should be generally prepared to handle any incident but should focus on being prepared to handle incidents that use common attack vectors.

Incidents can occur in countless ways, so it is infeasible to develop step-by-step instructions for handling every incident. This publication defines several types of incidents, based on common attack vectors; these categories are not intended to provide definitive classification for incidents, but rather to be used as a basis for defining more specific handling procedures. Different types of incidents merit different response strategies. The attack vectors are:

- **External/Removable Media:** An attack executed from removable media (e.g., flash drive, CD) or a peripheral device.
- **Attrition:** An attack that employs brute force methods to compromise, degrade, or destroy systems, networks, or services.
- **Web:** An attack executed from a website or web-based application.
- **Email:** An attack executed via an email message or attachment.
- **Improper Usage:** Any incident resulting from violation of an organization's acceptable usage policies by an authorized user, excluding the above categories.
- **Loss or Theft of Equipment:** The loss or theft of a computing device or media used by the organization, such as a laptop or smartphone.
- **Other:** An attack that does not fit into any of the other categories.

Organizations should emphasize the importance of incident detection and analysis throughout the organization.

In an organization, millions of possible signs of incidents may occur each day, recorded mainly by logging and computer security software. Automation is needed to perform an initial analysis of the data and select events of interest for human review. Event correlation software can be of great value in automating the analysis process. However, the effectiveness of the process depends on the quality of the data that goes into it. Organizations should establish logging standards and procedures to ensure that adequate information is collected by logs and security software and that the data is reviewed regularly.

Organizations should create written guidelines for prioritizing incidents.

Prioritizing the handling of individual incidents is a critical decision point in the incident response process. Effective information sharing can help an organization identify situations that are of greater severity and demand immediate attention. Incidents should be prioritized based on the relevant factors, such as the functional impact of the incident (e.g., current and likely future negative impact to business functions), the information impact of the incident (e.g., effect on the confidentiality, integrity, and availability of the organization's information), and the recoverability from the incident (e.g., the time and types of resources that must be spent on recovering from the incident).

Organizations should use the lessons learned process to gain value from incidents.

After a major incident has been handled, the organization should hold a lessons learned meeting to review the effectiveness of the incident handling process and identify necessary improvements to existing security controls and practices. Lessons learned meetings can also be held periodically for lesser incidents as time and resources permit. The information accumulated from all lessons learned meetings should be used to identify and correct systemic weaknesses and deficiencies in policies and procedures. Follow-up reports generated for each resolved incident can be important not only for evidentiary purposes but also for reference in handling future incidents and in training new team members.

In an organization, millions of possible signs of incidents may occur each day, recorded mainly by logging and computer security software. Automation is needed to perform an initial analysis of the data and select events of interest for human review. Event correlation software can be of great value in automating the analysis process. However, the effectiveness of the process depends on the quality of the data that goes into it. Organizations should establish logging standards and procedures to ensure that adequate information is collected by logs and security software and that the data is reviewed regularly.

1. Introduction

1.1. Authority

The National Institute of Standards and Technology (NIST) developed this document in furtherance of its statutory responsibilities under the Federal

Information Security Management Act (FISMA) of 2002, Public Law 107-347.

NIST is responsible for developing standards and guidelines, including minimum requirements, for providing adequate information security for all agency operations and assets, but such standards and guidelines shall not apply to national security systems. This guideline is consistent with the requirements of the Office of Management and Budget (OMB) Circular A-130, Section 8b(3), "Securing Agency Information Systems," as analyzed in A-130, Appendix IV: Analysis of Key Sections. Supplemental information is provided in A-130, Appendix III.

This guideline has been prepared for use by Federal agencies. It may be used by nongovernmental organizations on a voluntary basis and is not subject to copyright, though attribution is desired.

Nothing in this document should be taken to contradict standards and guidelines made mandatory and binding on Federal agencies by the Secretary of Commerce under statutory authority, nor should these guidelines be interpreted as altering or superseding the existing authorities of the Secretary of Commerce, Director of the OMB, or any other Federal official.

1.2. Purpose and Scope

This publication seeks to assist organizations in mitigating the risks from computer security incidents by providing practical guidelines on responding to incidents effectively and efficiently. It includes guidelines on establishing an effective incident response program, but the primary focus of the document is detecting, analyzing, prioritizing, and handling incidents. Organizations are encouraged to tailor the recommended guidelines and solutions to meet their specific security and mission requirements.

1.3. Audience

This document has been created for computer security incident response teams (CSIRTs), system and network administrators, security staff, technical support staff, chief information security officers (CISOs), chief information officers (CIOs), computer security program managers, and others who are responsible for preparing for, or responding to, security incidents.

1.4. Document Structure

The remainder of this document is organized into the following sections and appendices:

- Section 2 discusses the need for incident response, outlines possible incident response team structures, and highlights other groups within an organization that may participate in incident handling.
- Section 3 reviews the basic incident handling steps and provides advice for performing incident handling more effectively, particularly incident detection and analysis.
- Section 4 examines the need for incident response coordination and information sharing.
- Appendix A contains incident response scenarios and questions for use in incident response tabletop discussions.
- Appendix B provides lists of suggested data fields to collect for each incident.
- Appendices C and D contain a glossary and acronym list, respectively.
- Appendix E identifies resources that may be useful in planning and performing incident response.
- Appendix F covers frequently asked questions about incident response.
- Appendix G lists the major steps to follow when handling a computer security incident-related crisis.
- Appendix H contains a change log listing significant changes since the previous revision.

2. Organizing a Computer Security Incident Response Capability

Organizing an effective computer security incident response capability (CSIRC) involves several major decisions and actions. One of the first considerations should be to create an organization-specific definition of the term "incident" so that the scope of the term is clear. The organization should decide what services the incident response team should provide, consider which team structures and models can provide those services, and select and implement one or more incident response teams. Incident response plan, policy, and procedure creation is an important part of establishing a team, so that incident response is performed effectively, efficiently, and consistently, and so that the team is empowered to do what needs to be done. The plan, policies, and procedures should reflect the team's interactions with other teams within the organization as well as with outside parties, such as law enforcement, the media, and other incident response organizations. This section provides not only guidelines that should be helpful to organizations that are establishing incident response capabilities, but also advice on maintaining and enhancing existing capabilities.

2.1. Events and Incidents

An *event* is any observable occurrence in a system or network. Events include a user connecting to a file share, a server receiving a request for a web page, a user sending email, and a firewall blocking a connection attempt. *Adverse events* are events with a negative consequence, such as system crashes, packet floods, unauthorized use of system privileges, unauthorized access to sensitive data, and execution of malware that destroys data. This guide addresses only adverse events that are computer security-related, not those caused by natural disasters, power failures, etc.

A *computer security incident* is a violation or imminent threat of violation[1] of computer security policies, acceptable use policies, or standard security practices. Examples of incidents[2] are:

- An attacker commands a botnet to send high volumes of connection requests to a web server, causing it to crash.
- Users are tricked into opening a "quarterly report" sent via email that is actually malware; running the tool has infected their computers and established connections with an external host.
- An attacker obtains sensitive data and threatens that the details will be released publicly if the organization does not pay a designated sum of money.
- A user provides or exposes sensitive information to others through peer-to-peer file sharing services.

2.2. Need for Incident Response

Attacks frequently compromise personal and business data, and it is critical to respond quickly and effectively when security breaches occur. The concept of computer security incident response has become widely accepted and implemented. One of the benefits of having an incident response capability is that it supports responding to incidents systematically (i.e., following a consistent incident handling methodology) so that the appropriate actions are taken. Incident response helps personnel to minimize loss or theft of information and disruption of services caused by incidents. Another benefit of incident response is the ability to use information gained during incident handling to better prepare for handling future incidents and to provide stronger protection for systems and data. An incident response capability also helps with dealing properly with legal issues that may arise during incidents.

Besides the business reasons to establish an incident response capability, Federal departments and agencies must comply with law, regulations, and policy directing a coordinated, effective defense against information security threats. Chief among these are the following:

- OMB's Circular No. A-130, Appendix III,[3] released in 2000, which directs Federal agencies to "ensure that there is a capability to provide help to users when a security incident occurs in the system and to share information concerning common vulnerabilities and threats. This capability shall share information with other organizations ... and should assist the agency in pursuing appropriate legal action, consistent with Department of Justice guidance."
- FISM A (from 2002),[4] which requires agencies to have "procedures for detecting, reporting, and responding to security incidents" and establishes a centralized Federal information security incident center, in part to:
  - "Provide timely technical assistance to operators of agency information systems ... including guidance on detecting and handling information security incidents ...
  - Compile and analyze information about incidents that threaten information security ...
  - Inform operators of agency information systems about current and potential information security threats, and vulnerabilities ...."
- Federal Information Processing Standards (FIPS) 200, *Minimum Security Requirements for Federal Information and Information*

Systems[5], March 2006, which specifies minimum security requirements for Federal information and information systems, including incident response. The specific requirements are defined in NIST Special Publication (SP) 800-53, *Recommended Security Controls for Federal Information Systems and Organizations.*

- OMB Memorandum M -07-16, *Safeguarding Against and Responding to the Breach of Personally Identifiable Information*[6], May 2007, which provides guidance on reporting security incidents that involve PII.

2.3. Incident Response Policy, Plan, and Procedure Creation

This section discusses policies, plans, and procedures related to incident response, with an emphasis on interactions with outside parties.

2.3.1. Policy Elements

Policy governing incident response is highly individualized to the organization. However, most policies include the same key elements:

- Statement of management commitment
- Purpose and objectives of the policy
- Scope of the policy (to whom and what it applies and under what circumstances)
- Definition of computer security incidents and related terms
- Organizational structure and definition of roles, responsibilities, and levels of authority; should include the authority of the incident response team to confiscate or disconnect equipment and to monitor suspicious activity, the requirements for reporting certain types of incidents, the requirements and guidelines for external communications and information sharing (e.g., what can be shared with whom, when, and over what channels), and the handoff and escalation points in the incident management process
- Prioritization or severity ratings of incidents
- Performance measures (as discussed in Section 3.4.2)
- Reporting and contact forms.

2.3.2. Plan Elements

Organizations should have a formal, focused, and coordinated approach to responding to incidents, including an incident response plan that provides the roadmap for implementing the incident response capability. Each organization needs a plan that meets its unique requirements, which relates to the organization's mission, size, structure, and functions. The plan should lay out the necessary resources and management support. The incident response plan should include the following elements:

- Mission
- Strategies and goals
- Senior management approval
- Organizational approach to incident response
- How the incident response team will communicate with the rest of the organization and with other organizations
- Metrics for measuring the incident response capability and its effectiveness
- Roadmap for maturing the incident response capability
- How the program fits into the overall organization.

The organization's mission, strategies, and goals for incident response should help in determining the structure of its incident response capability. The incident response program structure should also be discussed within the plan. Section 2.4.1 discusses the types of structures.

Once an organization develops a plan and gains management approval, the organization should implement the plan and review it at least annually to ensure the organization is following the roadmap for maturing the capability and fulfilling their goals for incident response.

2.3.3. Procedure Elements

Procedures should be based on the incident response policy and plan. Standard operating procedures (SOPs) are a delineation of the specific technical processes, techniques, checklists, and forms used by the incident response team. SOPs should be reasonably comprehensive and detailed to ensure that the priorities of the organization are reflected in response operations. In addition, following standardized responses should minimize errors, particularly those that might be caused by stressful incident handling situations. SOPs should be tested to validate their accuracy and usefulness, then distributed to all team members. Training should be provided for SOP users; the SOP documents can be used as an instructional tool. Suggested SOP elements are presented throughout Section 3.

2.3.4. Sharing Information with Outside Parties

Organizations often need to communicate with outside parties regarding an incident, and they should do so whenever appropriate, such as contacting law enforcement, fielding media inquiries, and seeking external expertise. Another example is discussing incidents with other involved parties, such as Internet service providers (ISPs), the vendor of vulnerable software, or other incident response teams. Organizations may also proactively share relevant incident indicator information with peers to improve detection and analysis of incidents. The incident response team should discuss information sharing with the organization's public affairs office, legal department, and management before an incident occurs to establish policies and procedures regarding information sharing. Otherwise, sensitive information regarding incidents may be provided to unauthorized parties, potentially leading to additional disruption and financial loss. The team should document all contacts and communications with outside parties for liability and evidentiary purposes.

Figure 2-1. Communications with Outside Parties.

The following sections provide guidelines on communicating with several types of outside parties, as depicted in Figure 2-1. The double-headed arrows indicate that either party may initiate communications. See Section 4 for additional information on communicating with outside parties, and see Section 2.4 for a discussion of communications involving incident response outsourcers.

2.3.4.1. The Media

The incident handling team should establish media communications procedures that comply with the organization's policies on media interaction and information disclosure.[7] For discussing incidents with the media, organizations often find it beneficial to designate a single point of contact (POC) and at least one backup contact. The following actions are recommended for preparing these designated contacts and should also be considered for preparing others who may be communicating with the media:

- Conduct training sessions on interacting with the media regarding incidents, which should include the importance of not revealing sensitive information, such as technical details of countermeasures that could assist other attackers, and the positive aspects of communicating important information to the public fully and effectively.
- Establish procedures to brief media contacts on the issues and sensitivities regarding a particular incident before discussing it with the media.
- Maintain a statement of the current status of the incident so that communications with the media are consistent and up-to-date.
- Remind all staff of the general procedures for handling media inquiries.
- Hold mock interviews and press conferences during incident handling exercises. The following are examples of questions to ask the media contact:
    - Who attacked you? Why?
    - When did it happen? How did it happen? Did this happen because you have poor security practices?
    - How widespread is this incident? What steps are you taking to determine what happened and to prevent future occurrences?

- What is the impact of this incident? Was any personally identifiable information (PII) exposed? What is the estimated cost of this incident?

2.3.4.2. Law Enforcement

One reason that many security-related incidents do not result in convictions is that some organizations do not properly contact law enforcement. Several levels of law enforcement are available to investigate incidents: for example, within the United States, Federal investigatory agencies (e.g., the Federal Bureau of Investigation [FBI] and the U.S. Secret Service), district attorney offices, state law enforcement, and local (e.g., county) law enforcement. Law enforcement agencies in other countries may also be involved, such as for attacks launched from or directed at locations outside the US. In addition, agencies have an Office of Inspector General (OIG) for investigation of violation of the law within each agency. The incident response team should become acquainted with its various law enforcement representatives before an incident occurs to discuss conditions under which incidents should be reported to them, how the reporting should be performed, what evidence should be collected, and how it should be collected.

Law enforcement should be contacted through designated individuals in a manner consistent with the requirements of the law and the organization's procedures. Many organizations prefer to appoint one incident response team member as the primary POC with law enforcement. This person should be familiar with the reporting procedures for all relevant law enforcement agencies and well prepared to recommend which agency, if any, should be contacted. Note that the organization typically should not contact multiple agencies because doing so might result in jurisdictional conflicts. The incident response team should understand what the potential jurisdictional issues are (e.g., physical location—an organization based in one state has a server located in a second state attacked from a system in a third state, being used remotely by an attacker in a fourth state).

2.3.4.3. Incident Reporting Organizations

FISMA requires Federal agencies to report incidents to the United States Computer Emergency Readiness Team (US-CERT),[8] which is a governmentwide incident response organization that assists Federal civilian agencies in their incident handling efforts. US-CERT does not replace existing agency response teams; rather, it augments the efforts of Federal civilian agencies by serving as a focal point for dealing with incidents. US-CERT analyzes the agency-provided information to identify trends and indicators of attacks; these are easier to discern when reviewing data from many organizations than when reviewing the data of a single organization.

Each agency must designate a primary and secondary POC with US-CERT and report all incidents consistent with the agency's incident response policy. Organizations should create a policy that states who is designated to report incidents and how the incidents should be reported. Requirements, categories, and timeframes for reporting incidents to US-CERT are on the US-CERT website.[9] All Federal agencies must ensure that their incident response procedures adhere to US-CERT's reporting requirements and that the procedures are followed properly.

All organizations are encouraged to report incidents to their appropriate CSIRTs. If an organization does not have its own CSIRT to contact, it can report incidents to other organizations, including Information Sharing and Analysis Centers (ISACs). One of the functions of these industry-specific private sector groups is to share important computer security-related information among their members. Several ISACs have been formed for industry sectors such as Communications, Electric Sector, Financial Services, Information Technology, and Research and Education.[10]

2.3.4.4. Other Outside Parties

An organization may want to discuss incidents with other groups, including those listed below. When reaching out to these external parties, an organization may want to work through US-CERT or its ISAC, as a "trusted introducer" to broker the relationship. It is likely that others are experiencing similar issues, and the trusted introducer can ensure that any such patterns are identified and taken into consideration.

- **Organization's ISP.** An organization may need assistance from its ISP in blocking a major network-based attack or tracing its origin.
- **Owners of Attacking Addresses.** If attacks are originating from an external organization's IP address space, incident handlers may want to talk to the designated security contacts for the organization to alert them to the activity or to ask them to collect evidence. It is highly recommended to coordinate such communications with US-CERT or an ISAC.
- **Software Vendors.** Incident handlers may want to speak to a software vendor about suspicious activity. This contact could include questions regarding the significance of certain log entries or known false

positives for certain intrusion detection signatures, where minimal information regarding the incident may need to be revealed. More information may need to be provided in some cases—for example, if a server appears to have been compromised through an unknown software vulnerability. Software vendors may also provide information on known threats (e.g., new attacks) to help organizations understand the current threat environment.

- **Other Incident Response Teams.** An organization may experience an incident that is similar to ones handled by other teams; proactively sharing information can facilitate more effective and efficient incident handling (e.g., providing advance warning, increasing preparedness, developing situational awareness). Groups such as the Forum of Incident Response and Security Teams (FIRST)[11], the Government Forum of Incident Response and Security Teams (GFIRST)[12], and the Anti-Phishing Working Group (APWG)[13] are not incident response teams, but they promote information sharing among incident response teams.
- **Affected External Parties.** An incident may affect external parties directly—for example, an outside organization may contact the organization and claim that one of the organization's users is attacking it. Another way in which external parties may be affected is if an attacker gains access to sensitive information regarding them, such as credit card information. In some jurisdictions, organizations are required to notify all parties that are affected by such an incident. Regardless of the circumstances, it is preferable for the organization to notify affected external parties of an incident before the media or other external organizations do so. Handlers should be careful to give out only appropriate information—the affected parties may request details about internal investigations that should not be revealed publicly.

OMB Memorandum M-07-16, *Safeguarding Against and Responding to the Breach of Personally Identifiable Information*, requires Federal agencies to develop and implement a breach notification policy for personally identifiable information (PII).[14] Incident handlers should understand how their incident handling actions should differ when a PII breach is suspected to have occurred, such as notifying additional parties or notifying parties within a shorter timeframe. Specific recommendations for PII breach notification policies are presented in

OMB Memorandum M-07-16. Also, the National Conference of State Legislatures has a list of state security breach notification laws.[15]

2.4. Incident Response Team Structure

An incident response team should be available for anyone who discovers or suspects that an incident involving the organization has occurred. One or more team members, depending on the magnitude of the incident and availability of personnel, will then handle the incident. The incident handlers analyze the incident data, determine the impact of the incident, and act appropriately to limit the damage and restore normal services. The incident response team's success depends on the participation and cooperation of individuals throughout the organization. This section identifies such individuals, discusses incident response team models, and provides advice on selecting an appropriate model.

2.4.1. Team Models

Possible structures for an incident response team include the following:

- **Central Incident Response Team.** A single incident response team handles incidents throughout the organization. This model is effective for small organizations and for organizations with minimal geographic diversity in terms of computing resources.
- **Distributed Incident Response Teams.** The organization has multiple incident response teams, each responsible for a particular logical or physical segment of the organization. This model is effective for large organizations (e.g., one team per division) and for organizations with major computing resources at distant locations (e.g., one team per geographic region, one team per major facility). However, the teams should be part of a single coordinated entity so that the incident response process is consistent across the organization and information is shared among teams. This is particularly important because multiple teams may see components of the same incident or may handle similar incidents.
- **Coordinating Team.** An incident response team provides advice to other teams without having authority over those teams—for example, a departmentwide team may assist individual agencies' teams. This model can be thought of as a CSIRT for CSIRTs. Because the focus

of this document is central and distributed CSIRTs, the coordinating team model is not addressed in detail in this document.[16]

Incident response teams can also use any of three staffing models:

- **Employees.** The organization performs all of its incident response work, with limited technical and administrative support from contractors.
- **Partially Outsourced.** The organization outsources portions of its incident response work.
  Section 2.4.2 discusses the major factors that should be considered with outsourcing. Although incident response duties can be divided among the organization and one or more outsourcers in many ways, a few arrangements have become commonplace:
  - The most prevalent arrangement is for the organization to outsource 24-hours-a-day, 7-days-aweek (24/7) monitoring of intrusion detection sensors, firewalls, and other security devices to an offsite managed security services provider (M SSP). The MSSP identifies and analyzes suspicious activity and reports each detected incident to the organization's incident response team.
  - Some organizations perform basic incident response work in-house and call on contractors to assist with handling incidents, particularly those that are more serious or widespread.
- **Fully Outsourced.** The organization completely outsources its incident response work, typically to an onsite contractor. This model is most likely to be used when the organization needs a full-time, onsite incident response team but does not have enough available, qualified employees. It is assumed that the organization will have employees supervising and overseeing the outsourcer's work.

2.4.2. Team Model Selection

When selecting appropriate structure and staffing models for an incident response team, organizations should consider the following factors:

- **The Need for 24/7 Availability.** Most organizations need incident response staff to be available 24/7. This typically means that incident handlers can be contacted by phone, but it can also mean that an onsite presence is required. Real-time availability is the best for incident response because the longer an incident lasts, the more potential there is for damage and loss. Real-time contact is often needed when working with other organizations—for example, tracing an attack back to its source.

- **Full-Time Versus Part-Time Team Members.** Organizations with limited funding, staffing, or incident response needs may have only part-time incident response team members, serving as more of a virtual incident response team. In this case, the incident response team can be thought of as a volunteer fire department. When an emergency occurs, the team members are contacted rapidly, and those who can assist do so. An existing group such as the IT help desk can act as a first POC for incident reporting. The help desk members can be trained to perform the initial investigation and data gathering and then alert the incident response team if it appears that a serious incident has occurred.
- **Employee Morale.** Incident response work is very stressful, as are the on-call responsibilities of most team members. This combination makes it easy for incident response team members to become overly stressed. Many organizations will also struggle to find willing, available, experienced, and properly skilled people to participate, particularly in 24-hour support. Segregating roles, particularly reducing the amount of administrative work that team members are responsible for performing, can be a significant boost to morale.
- **Cost.** Cost is a major factor, especially if employees are required to be onsite 24/7. Organizations may fail to include incident response-specific costs in budgets, such as sufficient funding for training and maintaining skills. Because the incident response team works with so many facets of IT, its members need much broader knowledge than most IT staff members. They must also understand how to use the tools of incident response, such as digital forensics software. Other costs that may be overlooked are physical security for the team's work areas and communications mechanisms.
- **Staff Expertise.** Incident handling requires specialized knowledge and experience in several technical areas; the breadth and depth of knowledge required varies based on the severity of the organization's risks. Outsourcers may possess deeper knowledge of intrusion detection, forensics, vulnerabilities, exploits, and other aspects of security than employees of the organization. Also, MSSPs may be able to correlate events among customers so that they can identify new threats more quickly than any individual customer could.

However, technical staff members within the organization usually have much better knowledge of the organization's environment than an outsourcer would, which can be beneficial in identifying false positives associated with organization-specific behavior and the criticality of targets. Section 2.4.3 contains additional information on recommended team member skills.

When considering outsourcing, organizations should keep these issues in mind:

- **Current and Future Quality of Work.** Organizations should consider not only the current quality (breadth and depth) of the outsourcer's work, but also efforts to ensure the quality of future work— for example, minimizing turnover and burnout and providing a solid training program for new employees. Organizations should think about how they could objectively assess the quality of the outsourcer's work.
- **Division of Responsibilities.** Organizations are often unwilling to give an outsourcer authority to make operational decisions for the environment (e.g., disconnecting a web server). It is important to document the appropriate actions for these decision points. For example, one partially outsourced model addresses this issue by having the outsourcer provide incident data to the organization's internal team, along with recommendations for further handling the incident. The internal team ultimately makes the operational decisions, with the outsourcer continuing to provide support as needed.
- **Sensitive Information Revealed to the Contractor.** Dividing incident response responsibilities and restricting access to sensitive information can limit this. For example, a contractor may determine what user ID was used in an incident (e.g., ID 123456) but not know what person is associated with the user ID. Employees can then take over the investigation. Non-disclosure agreements (NDAs) are one possible option for protecting the disclosure of sensitive information.
- **Lack of Organization-Specific Knowledge.** Accurate analysis and prioritization of incidents are dependent on specific knowledge of the organization's environment. The organization should provide the outsourcer regularly updated documents that define what incidents it is concerned about, which resources are critical, and what the level of

response should be under various sets of circumstances. The organization should also report all changes and updates made to its IT infrastructure, network configuration, and systems. Otherwise, the contractor has to make a best guess as to how each incident should be handled, inevitably leading to mishandled incidents and frustration on both sides. Lack of organization-specific knowledge can also be a problem when incident response is not outsourced if communications are weak among teams or if the organization simply does not collect the necessary information.

- **Lack of Correlation.** Correlation among multiple data sources is very important. If the intrusion detection system records an attempted attack against a web server, but the outsourcer has no access to the server's logs, it may be unable to determine whether the attack was successful. To be efficient, the outsourcer will require administrative privileges to critical systems and security device logs remotely over a secure channel. This will increase administration costs, introduce additional access entry points, and increase the risk of unauthorized disclosure of sensitive information.
- **Handling Incidents at Multiple Locations.** Effective incident response work often requires a physical presence at the organization's facilities. If the outsourcer is offsite, consider where the outsourcer is located, how quickly it can have an incident response team at any facility, and how much this will cost. Consider onsite visits; perhaps there are certain facilities or areas where the outsourcer should not be permitted to work.
- **Maintaining Incident Response Skills In-House.** Organizations that completely outsource incident response should strive to maintain basic incident response skills in-house. Situations may arise in which the outsourcer is unavailable, so the organization should be prepared to perform its own incident handling. The organization's technical staff must also be able to understand the significance, technical implications, and impact of the outsourcer's recommendations.

2.4.3. Incident Response Personnel

A single employee, with one or more designated alternates, should be in charge of incident response. In a fully outsourced model, this person oversees and evaluates the outsourcer's work. All other models generally have a team manager and one or more deputies who assumes authority in the absence of the team manager. The managers typically perform a variety of tasks, including acting as a liaison with upper management and other teams and organizations, defusing crisis situations, and ensuring that the team has the necessary personnel, resources, and skills. Managers should be technically adept and have excellent communication skills, particularly an ability to communicate to a range of audiences. Managers are ultimately responsible for ensuring that incident response activities are performed properly.

In addition to the team manager and deputy, some teams also have a technical lead—a person with strong technical skills and incident response experience who assumes oversight of and final responsibility for the quality of the team's technical work. The position of technical lead should not be confused with the position of incident lead. Larger teams often assign an incident lead as the primary POC for handling a specific incident; the incident lead is held accountable for the incident's handling. Depending on the size of the incident response team and the magnitude of the incident, the incident lead may not actually perform any actual incident handling, but rather coordinate the handlers' activities, gather information from the handlers, provide incident updates to other groups, and ensure that the team's needs are met.

Members of the incident response team should have excellent technical skills, such as system administration, network administration, programming, technical support, or intrusion detection. Every team member should have good problem solving skills and critical thinking abilities. It is not necessary for every team member to be a technical expert—to a large degree, practical and funding considerations will dictate this—but having at least one highly proficient person in each major area of technology (e.g., commonly attacked operating systems and applications) is a necessity. It may also be helpful to have some team members specialize in particular technical areas, such as network intrusion detection, malware analysis, or forensics. It is also often helpful to temporarily bring in technical specialists that aren't normally part of the team.

It is important to counteract staff burnout by providing opportunities for learning and growth. Suggestions for building and maintaining skills are as follows:

- Budget enough funding to maintain, enhance, and expand proficiency in technical areas and security disciplines, as well as less technical topics such as the legal aspects of incident response. This should include sending staff to conferences and encouraging or otherwise incentivizing participation in conferences, ensuring the availability of technical references that promote deeper technical understanding, and occasionally bringing in outside experts (e.g., contractors) with deep technical knowledge in needed areas as funding permits.

- Give team members opportunities to perform other tasks, such as creating educational materials, conducting security awareness workshops, and performing research.
- Consider rotating staff members in and out of the incident response team, and participate in exchanges in which team members temporarily trade places with others (e.g., network administrators) to gain new technical skills.
- Maintain sufficient staffing so that team members can have uninterrupted time off work (e.g., vacations).
- Create a mentoring program to enable senior technical staff to help less experienced staff learn incident handling.
- Develop incident handling scenarios and have the team members discuss how they would handle them. Appendix A contains a set of scenarios and a list of questions to be used during scenario discussions.

Incident response team members should have other skills in addition to technical expertise. Teamwork skills are of fundamental importance because cooperation and coordination are necessary for successful incident response. Every team member should also have good communication skills. Speaking skills are important because the team will interact with a wide variety of people, and writing skills are important when team members are preparing advisories and procedures. Although not everyone within a team needs to have strong writing and speaking skills, at least a few people within every team should possess them so the team can represent itself well in front of others.

2.4.4. Dependencies within Organizations

It is important to identify other groups within the organization that may need to participate in incident handling so that their cooperation can be solicited before it is needed. Every incident response team relies on the expertise, judgment, and abilities of others, including:

- **Management.** Management establishes incident response policy, budget, and staffing. Ultimately, management is held responsible for coordinating incident response among various stakeholders, minimizing damage, and reporting to Congress, OM B, the General Accounting Office (GAO), and other parties.

- **Information Assurance.** Information security staff members may be needed during certain stages of incident handling (prevention, containment, eradication, and recovery)—for example, to alter network security controls (e.g., firewall rulesets).
- **IT Support.** IT technical experts (e.g., system and network administrators) not only have the needed skills to assist but also usually have the best understanding of the technology they manage on a daily basis. This understanding can ensure that the appropriate actions are taken for the affected system, such as whether to disconnect an attacked system.
- **Legal Department.** Legal experts should review incident response plans, policies, and procedures to ensure their compliance with law and Federal guidance, including the right to privacy. In addition, the guidance of the general counsel or legal department should be sought if there is reason to believe that an incident may have legal ramifications, including evidence collection, prosecution of a suspect, or a lawsuit, or if there may be a need for a memorandum of understanding (MOU) or other binding agreements involving liability limitations for information sharing.
- **Public Affairs and Media Relations.** Depending on the nature and impact of an incident, a need may exist to inform the media and, by extension, the public.
- **Human Resources.** If an employee is suspected of causing an incident, the human resources department may be involved—for example, in assisting with disciplinary proceedings.
- **Business Continuity Planning.** Organizations should ensure that incident response policies and procedures and business continuity processes are in sync. Computer security incidents undermine the business resilience of an organization. Business continuity planning professionals should be made aware of incidents and their impacts so they can fine-tune business impact assessments, risk assessments, and continuity of operations plans. Further, because business continuity planners have extensive expertise in minimizing operational disruption during severe circumstances, they may be valuable in planning responses to certain situations, such as denial of service (DoS) conditions.
- **Physical Security and Facilities Management.** Some computer security incidents occur through breaches of physical security or involve coordinated logical and physical attacks. The incident

response team also may need access to facilities during incident handling—for example, to acquire a compromised workstation from a locked office.

2.5. Incident Response Team Services

The main focus of an incident response team is performing incident response, but it is fairly rare for a team to perform incident response only. The following are examples of other services a team might offer:

- **Intrusion Detection.** The first tier of an incident response team often assumes responsibility for intrusion detection.[17] The team generally benefits because it should be poised to analyze incidents more quickly and accurately, based on the knowledge it gains of intrusion detection technologies.
- **Advisory Distribution.** A team may issue advisories within the organization regarding new vulnerabilities and threats.[18] Automated methods should be used whenever appropriate to disseminate information; for example, the National Vulnerability Database (NVD) provides information via XML and RSS feeds when new vulnerabilities are added to it.[19] Advisories are often most necessary when new threats are emerging, such as a high-profile social or political event (e.g., celebrity wedding) that attackers are likely to leverage in their social engineering. Only one group within the organization should distribute computer security advisories to avoid duplicated effort and conflicting information.
- **Education and Awareness.** Education and awareness are resource multipliers—the more the users and technical staff know about detecting, reporting, and responding to incidents, the less drain there should be on the incident response team. This information can be communicated through many means: workshops, websites, newsletters, posters, and even stickers on monitors and laptops.
- **Information Sharing.** Incident response teams often participate in information sharing groups, such as ISA Cs or regional partnerships. Accordingly, incident response teams often manage the organization's incident information sharing efforts, such as aggregating information related to incidents and effectively sharing that information with other

organizations, as well as ensuring that pertinent information is shared within the enterprise.

2.6. Recommendations

The key recommendations presented in this section for organizing a computer security incident handling capability are summarized below.

- **Establish a formal incident response capability.** Organizations should be prepared to respond quickly and effectively when computer security defenses are breached. FISM A requires Federal agencies to establish incident response capabilities.
- **Create an incident response policy.** The incident response policy is the foundation of the incident response program. It defines which events are considered incidents, establishes the organizational structure for incident response, defines roles and responsibilities, and lists the requirements for reporting incidents, among other items.
- **Develop an incident response plan based on the incident response policy.** The incident response plan provides a roadmap for implementing an incident response program based on the organization's policy. The plan indicates both short- and long-term goals for the program, including metrics for measuring the program. The incident response plan should also indicate how often incident handlers should be trained and the requirements for incident handlers.
- **Develop incident response procedures.** The incident response procedures provide detailed steps for responding to an incident. The procedures should cover all the phases of the incident response process. The procedures should be based on the incident response policy and plan.
- **Establish policies and procedures regarding incident-related information sharing.** The organization should communicate appropriate incident details with outside parties, such as the media, law enforcement agencies, and incident reporting organizations. The incident response team should discuss this with the organization's public affairs office, legal department, and management to establish policies and procedures regarding information sharing. The team should comply with existing organization policy on interacting with the media and other outside parties.

- **Provide pertinent information on incidents to the appropriate organization.** Federal civilian agencies are required to report incidents to US-CERT; other organizations can contact US-CERT and/or their ISAC. Reporting is beneficial because US-CERT and the ISA Cs use the reported data to provide information tD the reporting parties regarding new threats and incident trends.
- **Consider the relevant factors when selecting an incident response team model.** Organizations should carefully weigh the advantages and disadvantages of each possible team structure model and staffing model in the context of the organization's needs and available resources.
- **Select people with appropriate skills for the incident response team.** The credibility and proficiency of the team depend to a large extent on the technical skills and critical thinking abilities of its members. Critical technical skills include system administration, network administration, programming, technical support, and intrusion detection. Teamwork and communications skills are also needed for effective incident handling. Necessary training should be provided to all team members.
- **Identify other groups within the organization that may need to participate in incident handling.** Every incident response team relies on the expertise, judgment, and abilities of other teams, including management, information assurance, IT support, legal, public affairs, and facilities management.
- **Determine which services the team should offer.** Although the main focus of the team is incident response, most teams perform additional functions. Examples include monitoring intrusion detection sensors, distributing security advisories, and educating users on security.

3. Handling an Incident

The incident response process has several phases. The initial phase involves establishing and training an incident response team, and acquiring the necessary tools and resources. During preparation, the organization also attempts to limit the number of incidents that will occur by selecting and implementing a set of controls based on the results of risk assessments. However, residual risk will inevitably persist after controls are implemented. Detection of security breaches is thus necessary to alert the organization whenever incidents occur. In keeping with the severity of the incident, the organization can mitigate the impact of the incident by containing it and ultimately recovering from it. During this phase, activity often cycles back to detection and analysis—for example, to see if additional hosts are infected by malware while eradicating a malware incident. After the incident is adequately handled, the organization issues a report that details the cause and cost of the incident and the steps the organization should take to prevent future incidents. This section describes the major phases of the incident response process—preparation, detection and analysis, containment, eradication and recovery, and post-incident activity—in detail. Figure 3-1 illustrates the incident response life cycle.

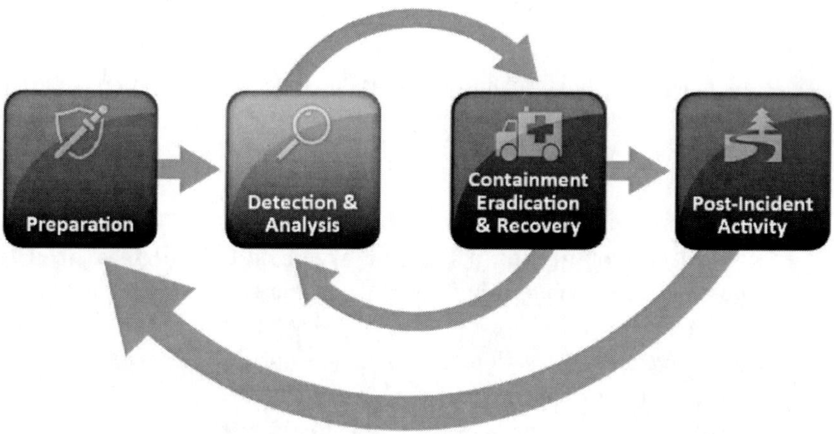

Figure 3-1. Incident Response Life Cycle.

3.1. Preparation

Incident response methodologies typically emphasize preparation—not only establishing an incident response capability so that the organization is ready to respond to incidents, but also preventing incidents by ensuring that systems, networks, and applications are sufficiently secure. Although the incident response team is not typically responsible for incident prevention, it is fundamental to the success of incident response programs. This section provides basic advice on preparing to handle incidents and on preventing incidents.

3.1.1. Preparing to Handle Incidents

The lists below provide examples of tools and resources available that may be of value during incident handling. These lists are intended to be a starting point for discussions about which tools and resources an organization's incident handlers need. For example, smartphones are one way to have resilient emergency communication and coordination mechanisms. An organization should have multiple (separate and different) communication and coordination mechanisms in case of failure of one mechanism.

Incident Handler Communications and Facilities

- **Contact information** for team members and others within and outside the organization (primary and backup contacts), such as law enforcement and other incident response teams; information may include phone numbers, email addresses, public encryption keys (in accordance with the encryption software described below), and instructions for verifying the contact's identity
- **On-call information** for other teams within the organization, including escalation information
- **Incident reporting mechanisms,** such as phone numbers, email addresses, online forms, and secure instant messaging systems that users can use to report suspected incidents; at least one mechanism should permit people to report incidents anonymously
- **Issue tracking system** for tracking incident information, status, etc.
- **Smartphones** to be carried by team members for off-hour support and onsite communications
- **Encryption software** to be used for communications among team members, within the organization and with external parties; for Federal agencies, software must use a FIPS-validated encryption al gorithm[20]
- **War room** for central communication and coordination; if a permanent war room is not necessary or practical, the team should create a procedure for procuring a temporary war room when needed
- **Secure storage facility** for securing evidence and other sensitive materials

Incident Analysis Hardware and Software

- **Digital forensic workstations[21] and/or backup devices** to create disk images, preserve log files, and save other relevant incident data

- **Laptops** for activities such as analyzing data, sniffing packets, and writing reports
- **Spare workstations, servers, and networking equipment, or the virtualized equivalents**, which may be used for many purposes, such as restoring backups and trying out mal ware
- **Blank removable media**
- **Portable printer** to print copies of log files and other evidence from non-networked systems
- **Packet sniffers and protocol analyzers** to capture and analyze network traffic
- **Digital forensic software** to analyze disk images
- **Removable media** with trusted versions of programs to be used to gather evidence from systems
- **Evidence gathering accessories**, including hard-bound notebooks, digital cameras, audio recorders, chain of custody forms, evidence storage bags and tags, and evidence tape, to preserve evidence for possible legal actions

Incident Analysis Resources

- **Port lists,** including commonly used ports and Trojan horse ports
- **Documentation** for OSs, applications, protocols, and intrusion detection and antivirus products
- **Network diagrams and lists of critical assets,** such as database servers
- **Current baselines** of expected network, system, and application activity
- **Cryptographic hashes** of critical files[22] to speed incident analysis, verification, and eradication

Incident Mitigation Software

- **Access to images** of clean OS and application installations for restoration and recovery purposes

Many incident response teams create a *jump kit*, which is a portable case that contains materials that may be needed during an investigation. The jump kit should be ready to go at all times. Jump kits contain many of the same items listed in the bulleted lists above. For example, each jump kit typically includes a laptop, loaded with appropriate software (e.g., packet sniffers, digital forensics). Other important materials include backup devices, blank media, and basic networking equipment and cables. Because the purpose of having a jump kit is to facilitate faster responses, the team should avoid borrowing items from the jump kit.

Each incident handler should have access to at least two computing devices (e.g., laptops). One, such as the one from the jump kit, should be used to perform packet sniffing, malware analysis, and all other actions that risk contaminating the laptop that performs them. This laptop should be scrubbed and all software reinstalled before it is used for another incident. Note that because this laptop is special purpose, it is likely to use software other than the standard enterprise tools and configurations, and whenever possible the incident handlers should be allowed to specify basic technical requirements for these special purpose investigative laptops. In addition to an investigative laptop, each incident handler should also have a standard laptop, smart phone, or other computing device for writing reports, reading email, and performing other duties unrelated to the hands-on incident analysis.

Exercises involving simulated incidents can also be very useful for preparing staff for incident handling; see NIST SP 800-84 for more information on exercises[23] and Appendix A for sample exercise scenarios.

3.1.2. Preventing Incidents

Keeping the number of incidents reasonably low is very important to protect the business processes of the organization. If security controls are insufficient, higher volumes of incidents may occur, overwhelming the incident response team. This can lead to slow and incomplete responses, which translate to a larger negative business impact (e.g., more extensive damage, longer periods of service and data unavailability).

It is outside the scope of this document to provide specific advice on securing networks, systems, and applications. Although incident response teams are generally not responsible for securing resources, they can be advocates of sound security practices. An incident response team may be able to identify problems that the organization is otherwise not aware of; the team can play a key role in risk assessment and training by identifying gaps. Other documents already provide advice on general security concepts and operating system and application-specific guidelines.[24] The following text, however, provides a brief overview of some of the main recommended practices for securing networks, systems, and applications:

- **Risk Assessments.** Periodic risk assessments of systems and applications should determine what risks are posed by combinations of threats and vulnerabilities.[25] This should include understanding the applicable threats, including organization-specific threats. Each risk should be prioritized, and the risks can be mitigated, transferred, or accepted until a reasonable overall level of risk is reached. Another benefit of conducting risk assessments regularly is that critical resources are identified, allowing staff to emphasize monitoring and response activities for those resources.[26]

- **Host Security.** All hosts should be hardened appropriately using standard configurations. In addition to keeping each host properly patched, hosts should be configured to follow the principle of least privilege—granting users only the privileges necessary for performing their authorized tasks. Hosts should have auditing enabled and should log significant security-related events. The security of hosts and their configurations should be continuously monitored.[27] Many organizations use Security Content Automation Protocol (SCAP)[28] expressed operating system and application configuration checklists to assist in securing hosts consistently and effectively.[29]
- **Network Security.** The network perimeter should be configured to deny all activity that is not expressly permitted. This includes securing all connection points, such as virtual private networks (V PNs) and dedicated connections to other organizations.
- **Malware Prevention.** Software to detect and stop malware should be deployed throughout the organization. Malware protection should be deployed at the host level (e.g., server and workstation operating systems), the application server level (e.g., email server, web proxies), and the application client level (e.g., email clients, instant messaging clients).[30]
- **User Awareness and Training.** Users should be made aware of policies and procedures regarding appropriate use of networks, systems, and applications. Applicable lessons learned from previous incidents should also be shared with users so they can see how their actions could affect the organization. Improving user awareness regarding incidents should reduce the frequency of incidents. IT staff should be trained so that they can maintain their networks, systems, and applications in accordance with the organization's security standards.

3.2. Detection and Analysis

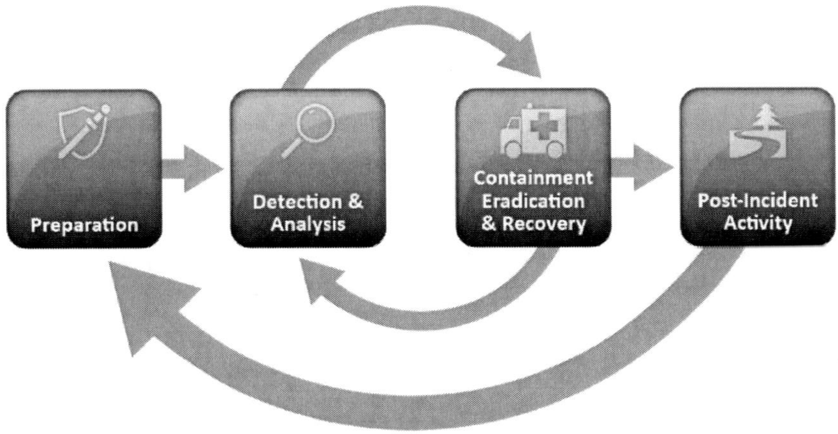

Figure 3-2. Incident Response Life Cycle (Detection and Analysis).

3.2.1. Attack Vectors

Incidents can occur in countless ways, so it is infeasible to develop step-by-step instructions for handling every incident. Organizations should be generally prepared to handle any incident but should focus on being prepared to handle incidents that use common attack vectors. Different types of incidents merit different response strategies. The attack vectors listed below are not intended to provide definitive classification for incidents; rather, they simply list common methods of attack, which can be used as a basis for defining more specific handling procedures.

- **External/Removable Media:** An attack executed from removable media or a peripheral device—for example, malicious code spreading onto a system from an infected USB flash drive.
- **Attrition:** An attack that employs brute force methods to compromise, degrade, or destroy systems, networks, or services (e.g., a DDoS intended to impair or deny access to a service or application; a brute force attack against an authentication mechanism, such as passwords, CAPTCHAS, or digital signatures).
- **Web:** An attack executed from a website or web-based application—for example, a cross-site scripting attack used to steal credentials or a redirect to a site that exploits a browser vulnerability and installs malware.

- **Email:** An attack executed via an email message or attachment—for example, exploit code disguised as an attached document or a link to a malicious website in the body of an email message.
- **Impersonation:** An attack involving replacement of something benign with something malicious— for example, spoofing, man in the middle attacks, rogue wireless access points, and SQL injection attacks all involve impersonation.
- **Improper Usage:** Any incident resulting from violation of an organization's acceptable usage policies by an authorized user, excluding the above categories; for example, a user installs file sharing software, leading to the loss of sensitive data; or a user performs illegal activities on a system.
- **Loss or Theft of Equipment:** The loss or theft of a computing device or media used by the organization, such as a laptop, smartphone, or authentication token.
- **Other:** An attack that does not fit into any of the other categories.

This section focuses on recommended practices for handling any type of incident. It is outside the scope of this publication to give specific advice based on the attack vectors; such guidelines would be provided in separate publications addressing other incident handling topics, such as NIST SP 800-83 on malware incident prevention and handling.

3.2.2. Signs of an Incident

For many organizations, the most challenging part of the incident response process is accurately detecting and assessing possible incidents—determining whether an incident has occurred and, if so, the type, extent, and magnitude of the problem. What makes this so challenging is a combination of three factors:

- Incidents may be detected through many different means, with varying levels of detail and fidelity. Automated detection capabilities include network-based and host-based IDPSs, antivirus software, and log analyzers. Incidents may also be detected through manual means, such as problems reported by users. Some incidents have overt signs that can be easily detected, whereas others are almost impossible to detect.
- The volume of potential signs of incidents is typically high—for example, it is not uncommon for an organization to receive thousands

or even millions of intrusion detection sensor alerts per day. (See Section 3.2.4 for information on analyzing such alerts.)

- Deep, specialized technical knowledge and extensive experience are necessary for proper and efficient analysis of incident-related data.

Signs of an incident fall into one of two categories: precursors and indicators. A *precursor* is a sign that an incident may occur in the future. An *indicator* is a sign that an incident may have occurred or may be occurring now.

Most attacks do not have any identifiable or detectable precursors from the target's perspective. If precursors are detected, the organization may have an opportunity to prevent the incident by altering its security posture to save a target from attack. At a minimum, the organization could monitor activity involving the target more closely. Examples of precursors are:

- Web server log entries that show the usage of a vulnerability scanner
- An announcement of a new exploit that targets a vulnerability of the organization's mail server
- A threat from a group stating that the group will attack the organization.

While precursors are relatively rare, indicators are all too common. Too many types of indicators exist to exhaustively list them, but some examples are listed below:

- A network intrusion detection sensor alerts when a buffer overflow attempt occurs against a database server.
- Antivirus software alerts when it detects that a host is infected with malware.
- A system administrator sees a filename with unusual characters.
- A host records an auditing configuration change in its log.
- An application logs multiple failed login attempts from an unfamiliar remote system.
- An email administrator sees a large number of bounced emails with suspicious content.
- A network administrator notices an unusual deviation from typical network traffic flows.

3.2.3. Sources of Precursors and Indicators

Precursors and indicators are identified using many different sources, with the most common being computer security software alerts, logs, publicly available information, and people. Table 3-2 lists common sources of precursors and indicators for each category.

Table 3-1. Common Sources of Precursors and Indicators

Source	Description
Alerts	
IDPSs	IDPS products identify suspicious events and record pertinent data regarding them, including the date and time the attack was detected, the type of attack, the source and destination IP addresses, and the username (if applicable and known). Most IDPS products use attack signatures to identify malicious activity; the signatures must be kept up to date so that the newest attacks can be detected. IDPS software often produces *false positives*—alerts that indicate malicious activity is occurring, when in fact there has been none. Analysts should manually validate IDPS alerts either by closely reviewing the recorded supporting data or by getting related data from other sources.[31]
SIEMs	Security Information and Event Management (SIEM) products are similar to IDPS products, but they generate alerts based on analysis of log data (see below).
Antivirus and antispam software	Antivirus software detects various forms of malware, generates alerts, and prevents the malware from infecting hosts. Current antivirus products are effective at stopping many instances of malware if their signatures are kept up to date. Antispam software is used to detect spam and prevent it from reaching users' mailboxes. Spam may contain malware, phishing attacks, and other malicious content, so alerts from antispam software may indicate attack attempts.
File integrity checking software	File integrity checking software can detect changes made to important files during incidents. It uses a hashing algorithm to obtain a cryptographic checksum for each designated file. If the file is altered and the checksum is recalculated, an extremely high probability exists that the new checksum will not match the old checksum. By regularly recalculating checksums and comparing them with previous values, changes to files can be detected.
Third-party monitoring services	Third parties offer a variety of subscription-based and free monitoring services. An example is fraud detection services that will notify an organization if its IP addresses, domain names, etc. are associated with current incident activity involving other organizations.

Source	Description
	There are also free real-time blacklists with similar information. Another example of a third-party monitoring service is a CSIRC notification list; these lists are often available only to other incident response teams.
Logs	
Operating system, service and application logs	Logs from operating systems, services, and applications (particularly audit-related data) are frequently of great value when an incident occurs, such as recording which accounts were accessed and what actions were performed. Organizations should require a baseline level of logging on all systems and a higher baseline level on critical systems. Logs can be used for analysis by correlating event information. Depending on the event information, an alert can be generated to indicate an incident. Section 3.2.4 discusses the value of centralized logging.
Network device logs	Logs from network devices such as firewalls and routers are not typically a primary source of precursors or indicators. Although these devices are usually configured to log blocked connection attempts, they provide little information about the nature of the activity. Still, they can be valuable in identifying network trends and in correlating events detected by other devices.
Network flows	A network flow is a particular communication session occurring between hosts. Routers and other networking devices can provide network flow information, which can be used to find anomalous network activity caused by malware, data exfiltration, and other malicious acts. There are many standards for flow data formats, including NetFlow, sFlow, and IPFIX.
Publicly Available Information	
Information on new vulnerabilities and exploits	Keeping up with new vulnerabilities and exploits can prevent some incidents from occurring and assist in detecting and analyzing new attacks. The National Vulnerability Database (NVD) contains information on vulnerabilities.[32] Organizations such as US-CERT[33] and CERT®/CC periodically provide threat update information through briefings, web postings, and mailing lists.
People	
People from within the organization	Users, system administrators, network administrators, security staff, and others from within the organization may report signs of incidents. It is important to validate all such reports. One approach is to ask people who provide such information how confident they are of the accuracy of the information. Recording this estimate along with the information provided can help considerably during incident analysis, particularly when conflicting data is discovered.

Table 3-1. (Continued)

Source	Description
People from other organizations	Reports of incidents that originate externally should be taken seriously. For example, the organization might be contacted by a party claiming a system at the organization is attacking its systems. External users may also report other indicators, such as a defaced web page or an unavailable service. Other incident response teams also may report incidents. It is important to have mechanisms in place for external parties to report indicators and for trained staff to monitor those mechanisms carefully; this may be as simple as setting up a phone number and email address, configured to forward messages to the help desk.

3.2.4. Incident Analysis

Incident detection and analysis would be easy if every precursor or indicator were guaranteed to be accurate; unfortunately, this is not the case. For example, user-provided indicators such as a complaint of a server being unavailable are often incorrect. Intrusion detection systems may produce false positives — incorrect indicators. These examples demonstrate what makes incident detection and analysis so difficult: each indicator ideally should be evaluated to determine if it is legitimate. Making matters worse, the total number of indicators may be thousands or millions a day. Finding the real security incidents that occurred out of all the indicators can be a daunting task.

Even if an indicator is accurate, it does not necessarily mean that an incident has occurred. Some indicators, such as a server crash or modification of critical files, could happen for several reasons other than a security incident, including human error. Given the occurrence of indicators, however, it is reasonable to suspect that an incident might be occurring and to act accordingly. Determining whether a particular event is actually an incident is sometimes a matter of judgment. It may be necessary to collaborate with other technical and information security personnel to make a decision. In many instances, a situation should be handled the same way regardless of whether it is security related. For example, if an organization is losing Internet connectivity every 12 hours and no one knows the cause, the staff would want to resolve the problem just as quickly and would use the same resources to diagnose the problem, regardless of its cause.

Some incidents are easy to detect, such as an obviously defaced web page. However, many incidents are not associated with such clear symptoms. Small signs such as one change in one system configuration file may be the only indicators that an incident has occurred. In incident handling, detection may be the most difficult task. Incident handlers are responsible for analyzing ambiguous, contradictory, and incomplete symptoms to determine what has happened. Although technical solutions exist that can make detection easier, the best remedy is to build a team of highly experienced and proficient staff members who can analyze the precursors and indicators effectively and efficiently and take appropriate actions. Without a well-trained and capable staff, incident detection and analysis will be conducted inefficiently, and costly mistakes will be made.

The incident response team should work quickly to analyze and validate each incident, following a predefined process and documenting each step taken. When the team believes that an incident has occurred, the team should rapidly perform an initial analysis to determine the incident's scope, such as which networks, systems, or applications are affected; who or what originated the incident; and how the incident is occurring (e.g., what tools or attack methods are being used, what vulnerabilities are being exploited). The initial analysis should provide enough information for the team to prioritize subsequent activities, such as containment of the incident and deeper analysis of the effects of the incident.

Performing the initial analysis and validation is challenging. The following are recommendations for making incident analysis easier and more effective:

- **Profile Networks and Systems.** *Profiling* is measuring the characteristics of expected activity so that changes to it can be more easily identified. Examples of profiling are running file integrity checking software on hosts to derive checksums for critical files and monitoring network bandwidth usage to determine what the average and peak usage levels are on various days and times. In practice, it is difficult to detect incidents accurately using most profiling techniques; organizations should use profiling as one of several detection and analysis techniques.
- **Understand Normal Behaviors.** Incident response team members should study networks, systems, and applications to understand what their normal behavior is so that abnormal behavior can be recognized more easily. No incident handler will have a comprehensive knowledge of all behavior throughout the environment, but handlers should know which experts could fill in the gaps. One way to gain this knowledge is through reviewing log entries and security alerts. This

may be tedious if filtering is not used to condense the logs to a reasonable size. As handlers become more familiar with the logs and alerts, they should be able to focus on unexplained entries, which are usually more important to investigate. Conducting frequent log reviews should keep the knowledge fresh, and the analyst should be able to notice trends and changes over time. The reviews also give the analyst an indication of the reliability of each source.

- **Create a Log Retention Policy.** Information regarding an incident may be recorded in several places, such as firewall, IDPS, and application logs. Creating and implementing a log retention policy that specifies how long log data should be maintained may be extremely helpful in analysis because older log entries may show reconnaissance activity or previous instances of similar attacks. Another reason for retaining logs is that incidents may not be discovered until days, weeks, or even months later. The length of time to maintain log data is dependent on several factors, including the organization's data retention policies and the volume of data. See N IST SP 800-92, *Guide to Computer Security Log Management* for additional recommendations related to logging.[34]
- **Perform Event Correlation.** Evidence of an incident may be captured in several logs that each contain different types of data—a firewall log may have the source IP address that was used, whereas an application log may contain a username. A network ID PS may detect that an attack was launched against a particular host, but it may not know if the attack was successful. The analyst may need to examine the host's logs to determine that information. Correlating events among multiple indicator sources can be invaluable in validating whether a particular incident occurred.
- **Keep All Host Clocks Synchronized.** Protocols such as the Network Time Protocol (NTP) synchronize clocks among hosts.[35] Event correlation will be more complicated if the devices reporting events have inconsistent clock settings. From an evidentiary standpoint, it is preferable to have consistent timestamps in logs—for example, to have three logs that show an attack occurred at 12:07:01 a.m., rather than logs that list the attack as occurring at 12:07:01, 12:10:35, and 11:07:06.
- **Maintain and Use a Knowledge Base of Information.** The knowledge base should include information that handlers need for referencing quickly during incident analysis. Although it is possible to

build a knowledge base with a complex structure, a simple approach can be effective. Text documents, spreadsheets, and relatively simple databases provide effective, flexible, and searchable mechanisms for sharing data among team members. The knowledge base should also contain a variety of information, including explanations of the significance and validity of precursors and indicators, such as ID PS alerts, operating system log entries, and application error codes.

- **Use Internet Search Engines for Research.** Internet search engines can help analysts find information on unusual activity. For example, an analyst may see some unusual connection attempts targeting TCP port 22912. Performing a search on the terms "TCP," "port," and "22912" may return some hits that contain logs of similar activity or even an explanation of the significance of the port number. Note that separate workstations should be used for research to minimize the risk to the organization from conducting these searches.
- **Run Packet Sniffers to Collect Additional Data.** Sometimes the indicators do not record enough detail to permit the handler to understand what is occurring. If an incident is occurring over a network, the fastest way to collect the necessary data may be to have a packet sniffer capture network traffic. Configuring the sniffer to record traffic that matches specified criteria should keep the volume of data manageable and minimize the inadvertent capture of other information. Because of privacy concerns, some organizations may require incident handlers to request and receive permission before using packet sniffers.
- **Filter the Data.** There is simply not enough time to review and analyze all the indicators; at mini mum the most suspicious activity should be investigated. One effective strategy is to filter out categories of indicators that tend to be insignificant. Another filtering strategy is to show only the categories of indicators that are of the highest significance; however, this approach carries substantial risk because new malicious activity may not fall into one of the chosen indicator categories.
- **Seek Assistance from Others.** Occasionally, the team will be unable to determine the full cause and nature of an incident. If the team lacks sufficient information to contain and eradicate the incident, then it should consult with internal resources (e.g., information security staff) and external resources (e.g., US-CERT, other CSIRTs, contractors with incident response expertise). It is important to accurately

determine the cause of each incident so that it can be fully contained and the exploited vulnerabilities can be mitigated to prevent similar incidents from occurring.

3.2.5. Incident Documentation

An incident response team that suspects that an incident has occurred should immediately start recording all facts regarding the incident.[36] A logbook is an effective and simple medium for this,[37] but laptops, audio recorders, and digital cameras can also serve this purpose.[38] Documenting system events, conversations, and observed changes in files can lead to a more efficient, more systematic, and less error-prone handling of the problem. Every step taken from the time the incident was detected to its final resolution should be documented and time stamped. Every document regarding the incident should be dated and signed by the incident handler. Information of this nature can also be used as evidence in a court of law if legal prosecution is pursued. Whenever possible, handlers should work in teams of at least two: one person can record and log events while the other person performs the technical tasks. Section 3.3.2 presents more information about evidence.[39]

The incident response team should maintain records about the status of incidents, along with other pertinent information.[40] Using an application or a database, such as an issue tracking system, helps ensure that incidents are handled and resolved in a timely manner. The issue tracking system should contain information on the following:

- The current status of the incident (new, i n progress, forwarded for investigation, resolved, etc.)
- A summary of the incident
- Indicators related to the incident
- Other incidents related to this incident
- Actions taken by all incident handlers on this incident
- Chain of custody, if applicable
- Impact assessments related to the incident
- Contact information for other involved parties (e.g., system owners, system administrators)
- A list of evidence gathered during the incident investigation
- Comments from incident handlers
- Next steps to be taken (e.g., rebuild the host, upgrade an application).[41]

The incident response team should safeguard incident data and restrict access to it because it often contains sensitive information—for example, data on exploited vulnerabilities, recent security breaches, and users that may have performed inappropriate actions. For example, only authorized personnel should have access to the incident database. Incident communications (e.g., emails) and documents should be encrypted or otherwise protected so that only authorized personnel can read them.

3.2.6. Incident Prioritization

Prioritizing the handling of the incident is perhaps the most critical decision point in the incident handling process. Incidents should not be handled on a first-come, first-served basis as a result of resource limitations. Instead, handling should be prioritized based on the relevant factors, such as the following:

- **Functional Impact of the Incident.** Incidents targeting IT systems typically impact the business functionality that those systems provide, resulting in some type of negative impact to the users of those systems. Incident handlers should consider how the incident will impact the existing functionality of the affected systems. Incident handlers should consider not only the current functional impact of the incident, but also the likely future functional impact of the incident if it is not immediately contained.
- **Information Impact of the Incident.** Incidents may affect the confidentiality, integrity, and availability of the organization's information. For example, a malicious agent may exfiltrate sensitive information. Incident handlers should consider how this information exfiltration will impact the organization's overall mission. An incident that results in the exfiltration of sensitive information may also affect other organizations if any of the data pertained to a partner organization.
- **Recoverability from the Incident.** The size of the incident and the type of resources it affects will determine the amount of time and resources that must be spent on recovering from that incident. In some instances it is not possible to recover from an incident (e.g., if the confidentiality of sensitive information has been compromised) and it would not make sense to spend limited resources on an elongated incident handling cycle, unless that effort was directed at ensuring that a similar incident did not occur in the future. In other cases, an

incident may require far more resources to handle than what an organization has available. Incident handlers should consider the effort necessary to actually recover from an incident and carefully weigh that against the value the recovery effort will create and any requirements related to incident handling.

Combining the functional impact to the organization's systems and the impact to the organization's information determines the business impact of the incident—for example, a distributed denial of service attack against a public web server may temporarily reduce the functionality for users attempting to access the server, whereas unauthorized root-level access to a public web server may result in the exfiltration of personally identifiable information (PII), which could have a long-lasting impact on the organization's reputation.

Table 3-2. Functional Impact Categories

Category	Definition
None	No effect to the organization's ability to provide all services to all users
Low	Minimal effect; the organization can still provide all critical services to all users but has lost efficiency
Medium	Organization has lost the ability to provide a critical service to a subset of system users
High	Organization is no longer able to provide some critical services to any users

The recoverability from the incident determines the possible responses that the team may take when handling the incident. An incident with a high functional impact and low effort to recover from is an ideal candidate for immediate action from the team. However, some incidents may not have smooth recovery paths and may need to be queued for a more strategic-level response—for example, an incident that results in an attacker exfiltrating and publicly posting gigabytes of sensitive data has no easy recovery path since the data is already exposed; in this case the team may transfer part of the responsibility for handling the data exfiltration incident to a more strategic-level team that develops strategy for preventing future breaches and creates an outreach plan for alerting those individuals or organizations whose data was exfiltrated. The team should prioritize the response to each incident based on its estimate of the business impact caused by the incident and the estimated efforts required to recover from the incident.

An organization can best quantify the effect of its own incidents because of its situational awareness. Table 3-2 provides examples of functional impact categories that an organization might use for rating its own incidents. Rating incidents can be helpful in prioritizing limited resources.

Table 3-3 provides examples of possible information impact categories that describe the extent of information compromise that occurred during the incident. In this table, with the exception of the 'None' value, the categories are not mutually exclusive and the organization could choose more than one.

Table 3-3. Information Impact Categories

Category	Definition
None	No information was exfiltrated, changed, deleted, or otherwise compromised
Privacy Breach	Sensitive personally identifiable information (PII) of taxpayers, employees, beneficiaries, etc. was accessed or exfiltrated
Proprietary Breach Integrity Loss	Unclassified proprietary information, such as protected critical infrastructure information (PCII), was accessed or exfiltrated Sensitive or proprietary information was changed or deleted

Table 3-4 shows examples of recoverability effort categories that reflect the level of and type of resources required to recover from the incident.

Table 3-4. Recoverability Effort Categories

Category	Definition
Regular	Time to recovery is predictable with existing resources
Supplemented	Time to recovery is predictable with additional resources
Extended	Time to recovery is unpredictable; additional resources and outside help are needed
Not Recoverable	Recovery from the incident is not possible (e.g., sensitive data exfiltrated and posted publicly); launch investigation

Organizations should also establish an escalation process for those instances when the team does not respond to an incident within the designated time. This can happen for many reasons: for example, cell phones may fail or people may have personal emergencies. The escalation process should state how long a person should wait for a response and what to do if no response occurs. Generally, the first step is to duplicate the initial contact. After waiting for a brief time—perhaps 15 minutes—the caller should escalate the incident to a higher level, such as the incident response team manager. If that person does not respond within a certain time, then the incident should be escalated again to a higher level of management. This process should be repeated until someone responds.

3.2.7. Incident Notification

When an incident is analyzed and prioritized, the incident response team needs to notify the appropriate individuals so that all who need to be involved will play their roles. Incident response policies should include provisions concerning incident reporting—at a minimum, what must be reported to whom and at what times (e.g., initial notification, regular status updates). The exact reporting requirements vary among organizations, but parties that are typically notified include:

- CIO
- Head of information security
- Local information security officer
- Other incident response teams within the organization
- External incident response teams (if appropriate)
- System owner
- Human resources (for cases involving employees, such as harassment through email)
- Public affairs (for incidents that may generate publicity)
- Legal department (for incidents with potential legal ramifications)
- US-CERT (required for Federal agencies and systems operated on behalf of the Federal government; see Section 2.3.4.3)
- Law enforcement (if appropriate)

During incident handling, the team may need to provide status updates to certain parties, even in some cases the entire organization. The team should plan and prepare several communication methods, including out-of-band methods (e.g., in person, paper), and select the methods that are appropriate for a particular incident. Possible communication methods include:

- Email
- Website (internal, external, or portal)
- Telephone calls
- In person (e.g., daily briefings)

- Voice mailbox greeting (e.g., set up a separate voice mailbox for incident updates, and update the greeting message to reflect the current incident status; use the help desk's voice mail greeting)
- Paper (e.g., post notices on bulletin boards and doors, hand out notices at all entrance points).

3.3. Containment, Eradication, and Recovery

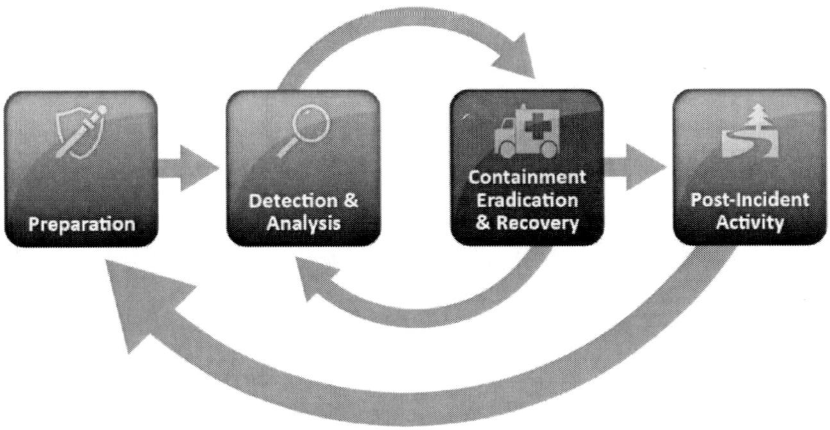

Figure 3-3. Incident Response Life Cycle (Containment, Eradication, and Recovery).

3.3.1. Choosing a Containment Strategy

Containment is important before an incident overwhelms resources or increases damage. Most incidents require containment, so that is an important consideration early in the course of handling each incident. Containment provides time for developing a tailored remediation strategy. An essential part of containment is decision-making (e.g., shut down a system, disconnect it from a network, disable certain functions). Such decisions are much easier to make if there are predetermined strategies and procedures for containing the incident. Organizations should define acceptable risks in dealing with incidents and develop strategies accordingly.

Containment strategies vary based on the type of incident. For example, the strategy for containing an email-borne malware infection is quite different from that of a network-based DDoS attack. Organizations should create separate containment strategies for each major incident type, with criteria documented clearly to facilitate decision-making. Criteria for determining the appropriate strategy include:

- Potential damage to and theft of resources
- Need for evidence preservation
- Service availability (e.g., network connectivity, services provided to external parties)
- Time and resources needed to implement the strategy
- Effectiveness of the strategy (e.g., partial containment, full containment)
- Duration of the solution (e.g., emergency workaround to be removed in four hours, temporary workaround to be removed in two weeks, permanent solution).

In certain cases, some organizations redirect the attacker to a sandbox (a form of containment) so that they can monitor the attacker's activity, usually to gather additional evidence. The incident response team should discuss this strategy with its legal department to determine if it is feasible. Ways of monitoring an attacker's activity other than sandboxing should not be used; if an organization knows that a system has been compromised and allows the compromise to continue, it may be liable if the attacker uses the compromised system to attack other systems. The delayed containment strategy is dangerous because an attacker could escalate unauthorized access or compromise other systems.

Another potential issue regarding containment is that some attacks may cause additional damage when they are contained. For example, a compromised host may run a malicious process that pings another host periodically. When the incident handler attempts to contain the incident by disconnecting the compromised host from the network, the subsequent pings will fail. As a result of the failure, the malicious process may overwrite or encrypt all the data on the host's hard drive. Handlers should not assume that just because a host has been disconnected from the network, further damage to the host has been prevented.

3.3.2. Evidence Gathering and Handling

Although the primary reason for gathering evidence during an incident is to resolve the incident, it may also be needed for legal proceedings.[42] In such cases, it is important to clearly document how all evidence, including compromised systems, has been preserved.[43] Evidence should be collected according to procedures that meet all applicable laws and regulations that have been developed from previous discussions with legal staff and appropriate law enforcement agencies so that any evidence can be admissible in court.[44] In addition, evidence should be accounted for at all times; whenever evidence is transferred from person to person, chain of custody forms should detail the transfer and include each party's signature. A detailed log should be kept for all evidence, including the following:

- Identifying information (e.g., the location, serial number, model number, hostname, media access control (MAC) addresses, and IP addresses of a computer)
- Name, title, and phone number of each individual who collected or handled the evidence during the investigation
- Time and date (including time zone) of each occurrence of evidence handling
- Locations where the evidence was stored.

Collecting evidence from computing resources presents some challenges. It is generally desirable to acquire evidence from a system of interest as soon as one suspects that an incident may have occurred. Many incidents cause a dynamic chain of events to occur; an initial system snapshot may do more good in identifying the problem and its source than most other actions that can be taken at this stage. From an evidentiary standpoint, it is much better to get a snapshot of the system as-is rather than doing so after incident handlers, system administrators, and others have inadvertently altered the state of the machine during the investigation. Users and system administrators should be made aware of the steps that they should take to preserve evidence. See NIST SP 800-86, *Guide to Integrating Forensic Techniques into Incident Response*, for additional information on preserving evidence.

3.3.3. Identifying the Attacking Hosts

During incident handling, system owners and others sometimes want to or need to identify the attacking host or hosts. Although this information can be important, incident handlers should generally stay focused on containment, eradication, and recovery. Identifying an attacking host can be a time-consuming and futile process that can prevent a team from achieving its primary goal—minimizing the business impact. The following items describe the most commonly performed activities for attacking host identification:

- **Validating the Attacking Host's IP Address.** New incident handlers often focus on the attacking host's IP address. The handler may attempt to validate that the address was not spoofed by verifying connectivity to it; however, this simply indicates that a host at that address does or does not respond to the requests. A failure to respond does not mean the address is not real—for example, a host may be configured to ignore pings and trace routes. Also, the attacker may have received a dynamic address that has already been reassigned to someone else.
- **Researching the Attacking Host through Search Engines.** Performing an Internet search using the apparent source IP address of an attack may lead to more information on the attack—for example, a mailing list message regarding a similar attack.
- **Using Incident Databases.** Several groups collect and consolidate incident data from various organizations into incident databases. This information sharing may take place in many forms, such as trackers and real-time blacklists. The organization can also check its own knowledge base or issue tracking system for related activity.
- **Monitoring Possible Attacker Communication Channels.** Incident handlers can monitor communication channels that may be used by an attacking host. For example, many bots use IRC as their primary means of communication. Also, attackers may congregate on certain IRC channels to brag about their compromises and share information. However, incident handlers should treat any such information that they acquire only as a potential lead, not as fact.

3.3.4. Eradication and Recovery

After an incident has been contained, eradication may be necessary to eliminate components of the incident, such as deleting malware and disabling breached user accounts, as well as identifying and mitigating all vulnerabilities that were exploited. During eradication, it is important to identify all affected hosts within the organization so that they can be remediated. For some incidents, eradication is either not necessary or is performed during recovery.

In recovery, administrators restore systems to normal operation, confirm that the systems are functioning normally, and (if applicable) remediate vulnerabilities to prevent similar incidents. Recovery may involve such actions as restoring systems from clean backups, rebuilding systems from scratch, replacing compromised files with clean versions, installing patches, changing passwords, and tightening network perimeter security (e.g., firewall rule sets, boundary router access control lists). Higher levels of system logging or network monitoring are often part of the recovery process. Once a resource is successfully attacked, it is often attacked again, or other resources within the organization are attacked in a similar manner.

Eradication and recovery should be done in a phased approach so that remediation steps are prioritized. For large-scale incidents, recovery may take months; the intent of the early phases should be to increase the overall security with relatively quick (days to weeks) high value changes to prevent future incidents. The later phases should focus on longer-term changes (e.g., infrastructure changes) and ongoing work to keep the enterprise as secure as possible.

Because eradication and recovery actions are typically OS or application-specific, detailed recommendations and advice regarding them are outside the scope of this document.

3.4. Post-Incident Activity

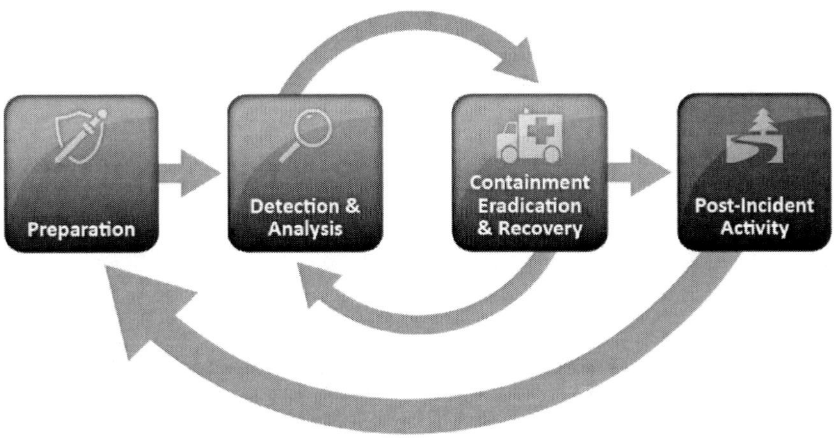

Figure 3-4. Incident Response Life Cycle (Post-Incident Activity).

3.4.1. Lessons Learned

One of the most important parts of incident response is also the most often omitted: learning and improving. Each incident response team should evolve to reflect new threats, improved technology, and lessons learned. Holding a "lessons learned" meeting with all involved parties after a major incident, and optionally periodically after lesser incidents as resources permit, can be extremely helpful in improving security measures and the incident handling process itself. Multiple incidents can be covered in a single lessons learned meeting. This meeting provides a chance to achieve closure with respect to an incident by reviewing what occurred, what was done to intervene, and how well intervention worked. The meeting should be held within several days of the end of the incident. Questions to be answered in the meeting include:

- Exactly what happened, and at what times?
- How well did staff and management perform in dealing with the incident? Were the documented procedures followed? Were they adequate?
- What information was needed sooner?
- Were any steps or actions taken that might have inhibited the recovery?
- What would the staff and management do differently the next time a similar incident occurs?
- How could information sharing with other organizations have been improved?
- What corrective actions can prevent similar incidents in the future?
- What precursors or indicators should be watched for in the future to detect similar incidents?
- What additional tools or resources are needed to detect, analyze, and mitigate future incidents?

Small incidents need limited post-incident analysis, with the exception of incidents performed through new attack methods that are of widespread concern and interest. After serious attacks have occurred, it is usually worthwhile to hold post-mortem meetings that cross team and organizational boundaries to provide a mechanism for information sharing. The primary consideration in holding such meetings is ensuring that the right people are involved. Not only is it important to invite people who have been involved in the incident that is being analyzed, but also it is wise to consider who should be invited for the purpose of facilitating future cooperation.

The success of such meetings also depends on the agenda. Collecting input about expectations and needs (including suggested topics to cover) from participants before the meeting increases the likelihood that the participants' needs will be met. In addition, establishing rules of order before or during the start of a meeting can minimize confusion and discord. Having one or more moderators who are skilled in group facilitation can yield a high payoff.

Finally, it is also important to document the major points of agreement and action items and to communicate them to parties who could not attend the meeting.

Lessons learned meetings provide other benefits. Reports from these meetings are good material for training new team members by showing them how more experienced team members respond to incidents. Updating incident response policies and procedures is another important part of the lessons learned process. Post-mortem analysis of the way an incident was handled will often reveal a missing step or an inaccuracy in a procedure, providing impetus for change. Because of the changing nature of information technology and changes in personnel, the incident response team should review all related documentation and procedures for handling incidents at designated intervals.

Another important post-incident activity is creating a follow-up report for each incident, which can be quite valuable for future use. The report provides a reference that can be used to assist in handling similar incidents. Creating a formal chronology of events (including time stamped information such as log data from systems) is important for legal reasons, as is creating a monetary estimate of the amount of damage the incident caused. This estimate may become the basis for subsequent prosecution activity by entities such as the U.S. Attorney General's office. Follow-up reports should be kept for a period of time as specified in record retention policies.[45]

3.4.2. Using Collected Incident Data

Lessons learned activities should produce a set of objective and subjective data regarding each incident. Over time, the collected incident data should be useful in several capacities. The data, particularly the total hours of involvement and the cost, may be used to justify additional funding of the incident response team. A study of incident characteristics may indicate systemic security weaknesses and threats, as well as changes in incident trends. This data can be put back into the risk assessment process, ultimately leading to the selection and implementation of additional controls. Another good use of the data is measuring the success of the incident response team. If incident data is collected and stored properly, it should provide several measures of the success (or at least the activities) of the incident response team. Incident data can also be collected to determine if a change to incident response capabilities causes a corresponding change in the team's performance (e.g., improvements in efficiency, reductions in costs). Furthermore, organizations that are required to report incident information will need to collect the necessary data to meet their requirements. See Section 4 for additional information on sharing incident data with other organizations.

Organizations should focus on collecting data that is actionable, rather than collecting data simply because it is available. For example, counting the number of precursor port scans that occur each week and producing a chart at the end of the year that shows port scans increased by eight percent is not very helpful and may be quite time-consuming. Absolute numbers are not informative—understanding how they represent threats to the business processes of the organization is what matters. Organizations should decide what incident data to collect based on reporting requirements and on the expected return on investment from the data (e.g., identifying a new threat and mitigating the related vulnerabilities before they can be exploited.) Possible metrics for incident-related data include:

- **Number of Incidents Handled.**[46] Handling more incidents is not necessarily better—for example, the number of incidents handled may decrease because of better network and host security controls, not because of negligence by the incident response team. The number of incidents handled is best taken as a measure of the relative amount of work that the incident response team had to perform, not as a measure of the quality of the team, unless it is considered in the context of other measures that collectively give an indication of work quality. It is more effective to produce separate incident counts for each incident category. Subcategories also can be used to provide more information. For example, a growing number of incidents performed by insiders could prompt stronger policy provisions concerning background investigations for personnel and misuse of computing resources and stronger security controls on internal networks (e.g., deploying intrusion detection software to more internal networks and hosts).
- **Time Per Incident.** For each incident, time can be measured in several ways:
  - Total amount of labor spent working on the incident
  - Elapsed time from the beginning of the incident to incident discovery, to the initial impact assessment, and to each stage of the incident handling process (e.g., containment, recovery)
  - How long it took the incident response team to respond to the initial report of the incident
  - How long it took to report the incident to management and, if necessary, appropriate external entities (e.g., US-CERT).

- **Objective Assessment of Each Incident.** The response to an incident that has been resolved can be analyzed to determine how effective it was. The following are examples of performing an objective assessment of an incident:
    - Reviewing logs, forms, reports, and other incident documentation for adherence to established incident response policies and procedures
    - Identifying which precursors and indicators of the incident were recorded to determine how effectively the incident was logged and identified
    - Determining if the incident caused damage before it was detected
    - Determining if the actual cause of the incident was identified, and identifying the vector of attack, the vulnerabilities exploited, and the characteristics of the targeted or victimized systems, networks, and applications
    - Determining if the incident is a recurrence of a previous incident
    - Calculating the estimated monetary damage from the incident (e.g., information and critical business processes negatively affected by the incident)
    - Measuring the difference between the initial impact assessment and the final impact assessment (see Section 3.2.6)
    - Identifying which measures, if any, could have prevented the incident.
- **Subjective Assessment of Each Incident.** Incident response team members may be asked to assess their own performance, as well as that of other team members and of the entire team. Another valuable source of input is the owner of a resource that was attacked, in order to determine if the owner thinks the incident was handled efficiently and if the outcome was satisfactory.

Besides using these metrics to measure the team's success, organizations may also find it useful to periodically audit their incident response programs. Audits will identify problems and deficiencies that can then be corrected. At a minimum, an incident response audit should evaluate the following items against applicable regulations, policies, and generally accepted practices:

- Incident response policies, plans, and procedures
- Tools and resources
- Team model and structure

- Incident handler training and education
- Incident documentation and reports
- The measures of success discussed earlier in this section.

3.4.3. Evidence Retention

Organizations should establish policy for how long evidence from an incident should be retained. Most organizations choose to retain all evidence for months or years after the incident ends. The following factors should be considered during the policy creation:

- **Prosecution.** If it is possible that the attacker will be prosecuted, evidence may need to be retained until all legal actions have been completed. In some cases, this may take several years. Furthermore, evidence that seems insignificant now may become more important in the future. For example, if an attacker is able to use knowledge gathered in one attack to perform a more severe attack later, evidence from the first attack may be key to explaining how the second attack was accomplished.
- **Data Retention.** Most organizations have data retention policies that state how long certain types of data may be kept. For example, an organization may state that email messages should be retained for only 180 days. If a disk image contains thousands of emails, the organization may not want the image to be kept for more than 180 days unless it is absolutely necessary. As discussed in Section 3.4.2, General Records Schedule (GRS) 24 specifies that incident handling records should be kept for three years.
- **Cost.** Original hardware (e.g., hard drives, compromised systems) that is stored as evidence, as well as hard drives and removable media that are used to hold disk images, are generally individually inexpensive. However, if an organization stores many such components for years, the cost can be substantial. The organization also must retain functional computers that can use the stored hardware and media.

3.5. Incident Handling Checklist

The checklist i n Table 3-6 provides the major steps to be performed in the handling of an incident. Note that the actual steps performed may vary based on the type of incident and the nature of individual incidents. For example, if the handler knows exactly what has happened based on analysis of indicators (Step 1.1), there may be no need to perform Steps 1.2 or 1.3 to further research the activity. The checklist provides guidelines to handlers on the major steps that should be performed; it does not dictate the exact sequence of steps that should always be followed.

Table 3-5. Incident Handling Checklist

Action		Compled
Detection and Analysis		
1.	Determine whether an incident has occurred	
1.1	Analyze the precursors and indicators	
1.2	Look for correlating information	
1.3	Perform research (e.g., search engines, knowledge base)	
1.4	As soon as the handler believes an incident has occurred, begin documenting the investigation and gathering evidence	
2.	Prioritize handling the incident based on the relevant factors (functional impact, information impact, recoverability effort, etc.)	
3.	Report the incident to the appropriate internal personnel and external organizations	
Containment, Eradication, and Recovery		
4.	Acquire, preserve, secure, and document evidence	
5.	Contain the incident	
6.	Eradicate the incident	
6.1	Identify and mitigate all vulnerabilities that were exploited	
6.2	Remove malware, inappropriate materials, and other components	
6.3	If more affected hosts are discovered (e.g., new malware infections), repeat the Detection and Analysis steps (1.1, 1.2) to identify all other affected hosts, then contain (5) and eradicate (6) the incident for them	
7.	Recover from the incident	
7.1	Return affected systems to an operationally ready state	
7.2	Confirm that the affected systems are functioning normally	
7.3	If necessary, implement additional monitoring to look for future related activity	
Post-Incident Activity		
8.	Create a follow-up report	
9.	Hold a lessons learned meeting (mandatory for major incidents, optional otherwise)	

3.6. Recommendations

The key recommendations presented in this section for handling incidents are summarized below.

- **Acquire tools and resources that may be of value during incident handling.** The team will be more efficient at handling incidents if various tools and resources are already available to them. Examples include contact lists, encryption software, network diagrams, backup devices, digital forensic software, and port lists.
- **Prevent incidents from occurring by ensuring that networks, systems, and applications are sufficiently secure.** Preventing incidents is beneficial to the organization and also reduces the workload of the incident response team. Performing periodic risk assessments and reducing the identified risks to an acceptable level are effective in reducing the number of incidents. Awareness of security policies and procedures by users, IT staff, and management is also very important.
- **Identify precursors and indicators through alerts generated by several types of security software.** Intrusion detection and prevention systems, antivirus software, and file integrity checking software are valuable for detecting signs of incidents. Each type of software may detect incidents that the other types of software cannot, so the use of several types of computer security software is highly recommended. Third-party monitoring services can also be helpful .
- **Establish mechanisms for outside parties to report incidents.** Outside parties may want to report incidents to the organization—for example, they may believe that one of the organization's users is attacking them. Organizations should publish a phone number and email address that outside parties can use to report such incidents.
- **Require a baseline level of logging and auditing on all systems, and a higher baseline level on all critical systems.** Logs from operating systems, services, and applications frequently provide value during incident analysis, particularly if auditing was enabled. The logs can provide information such as which accounts were accessed and what actions were performed.
- **Profile networks and systems.** Profiling measures the characteristics of expected activity levels so that changes in patterns can be more easily identified. If the profiling process is automated, deviations from

expected activity levels can be detected and reported to administrators quickly, leading to faster detection of incidents and operational issues.

- **Understand the normal behaviors of networks, systems, and applications.** Team members who understand normal behavior should be able to recognize abnormal behavior more easily. This knowledge can best be gained by reviewing log entries and security alerts; the handlers should become familiar with the typical data and can investigate the unusual entries to gain more knowledge.
- **Create a log retention policy.** Information regarding an incident may be recorded in several places. Creating and implementing a log retention policy that specifies how long log data should be maintained may be extremely helpful in analysis because older log entries may show reconnaissance activity or previous instances of similar attacks.
- **Perform event correlation.** Evidence of an incident may be captured in several logs. Correlating events among multiple sources can be invaluable in collecting all the available information for an incident and validating whether the incident occurred.
- **Keep all host clocks synchronized.** If the devices reporting events have inconsistent clock settings, event correlation will be more complicated. Clock discrepancies may also cause issues from an evidentiary standpoint.
- **Maintain and use a knowledge base of information.** Handlers need to reference information quickly during incident analysis; a centralized knowledge base provides a consistent, maintainable source of information. The knowledge base should include general information, such as data on precursors and indicators of previous incidents.
- **Start recording all information as soon as the team suspects that an incident has occurred.** Every step taken, from the time the incident was detected to its final resolution, should be documented and time stamped. Information of this nature can serve as evidence in a court of law if legal prosecution is pursued. Recording the steps performed can also lead to a more efficient, systematic, and less error-prone handling of the problem.
- **Safeguard incident data.** It often contains sensitive information regarding such things as vulnerabilities, security breaches, and users that may have performed inappropriate actions. The team should ensure that access to incident data is restricted properly, both logically and physically.

- **Prioritize handling of the incidents based on the relevant factors.** Because of resource limitations, incidents should not be handled on a first-come, first-served basis. Instead, organizations should establish written guidelines that outline how quickly the team must respond to the incident and what actions should be performed, based on relevant factors such as the functional and information impact of the incident, and the likely recoverability from the incident. This saves time for the incident handlers and provides a justification to management and system owners for their actions. Organizations should also establish an escalation process for those instances when the team does not respond to an incident within the designated time.
- **Include provisions regarding incident reporting in the organization's incident response policy.** Organizations should specify which incidents must be reported, when they must be reported, and to whom. The parties most commonly notified are the CIO, head of information security, local information security officer, other incident response teams within the organization, and system owners.
- **Establish strategies and procedures for containing incidents.** It is important to contain incidents quickly and effectively to limit their business impact. Organizations should define acceptable risks in containing incidents and develop strategies and procedures accordingly. Containment strategies should vary based on the type of incident.
- **Follow established procedures for evidence gathering and handling.** The team should clearly document how all evidence has been preserved. Evidence should be accounted for at all times. The team should meet with legal staff and law enforcement agencies to discuss evidence handling, then develop procedures based on those discussions.
- **Capture volatile data from systems as evidence.** This includes lists of network connections, processes, login sessions, open files, network interface configurations, and the contents of memory. Running carefully chosen commands from trusted media can collect the necessary information without damaging the system's evidence.
- **Obtain system snapshots through full forensic disk images, not file system backups.** Disk i mages should be made to sanitized write-protectable or write-once media. This process is superior to a file system backup for investigatory and evidentiary purposes. Imaging is

also valuable in that it is much safer to analyze an image than it is to perform analysis on the original system because the analysis may inadvertently alter the original.

- **Hold lessons learned meetings after major incidents.** Lessons learned meetings are extremely helpful in improving security measures and the incident handling process itself.

4. Coordination and Information Sharing

The nature of contemporary threats and attacks makes it more important than ever for organizations to work together during incident response. Organizations should ensure that they effectively coordinate portions of their incident response activities with appropriate partners. The most important aspect of incident response coordination is information sharing, where different organizations share threat, attack, and vulnerability information with each other so that each organization's knowledge benefits the other. Incident information sharing is frequently mutually beneficial because the same threats and attacks often affect multiple organizations simultaneously.

As mentioned in Section 2, coordinating and sharing information with partner organizations can strengthen the organization's ability to effectively respond to IT incidents. For example, if an organization identifies some behavior on its network that seems suspicious and sends information about the event to a set of trusted partners, someone else in that network may have already seen similar behavior and be able to respond with additional details about the suspicious activity, including signatures, other indicators to look for, or suggested remediation actions. Collaboration with the trusted partner can enable an organization to respond to the incident more quickly and efficiently than an organization operating in isolation.

This increase in efficiency for standard incident response techniques is not the only incentive for cross-organization coordination and information sharing. Another incentive for information sharing is the ability to respond to incidents using techniques that may not be available to a single organization, especially if that organization is small to medium size. For example, a small organization that identifies a particularly complex instance of malware on its network may not have the in-house resources to fully analyze the malware and determine its effect on the system. In this case, the organization may be able to leverage a trusted information sharing network to effectively outsource the analysis of this malware to third party resources that have the adequate technical capabilities to perform the malware analysis.

This section of the document highlights coordination and information sharing. Section 4.1 presents an overview of incident response coordination and focuses on the need for cross-organization coordination to supplement organization incident response processes. Section 4.2 discusses techniques for information sharing across organizations, and Section 4.3 examines how to restrict what information is shared or not shared with other organizations.

4.1. Coordination

As discussed in Section 2.3.4, an organization may need to interact with several types of external organizations in the course of conducting incident response activities. Examples of these organizations include other incident response teams, law enforcement agencies, Internet service providers, and constituents and customers. An organization's incident response team should plan its incident coordination with those parties before incidents occur to ensure that all parties know their roles and that effective lines of communication are established. Figure 4-1 provides a sample view into an organization performing coordination at every phase of the incident response lifecycle, highlighting that coordination is valuable throughout the lifecycle.

4.1.1. Coordination Relationships

An incident response team within an organization may participate in different types of coordination arrangements, depending on the type of organization with which it is coordinating. For example, the team members responsible for the technical details of incident response may coordinate with operational colleagues at partner organizations to share strategies for mitigating an attack spanning multiple organizations. Alternatively, during the same incident, the incident response team manager may coordinate with ISACs to satisfy necessary reporting requirements and seek advice and additional resources for successfully responding to the incident. Table 4-1 provides some examples of coordination relationships that may exist when collaborating with outside organizations.

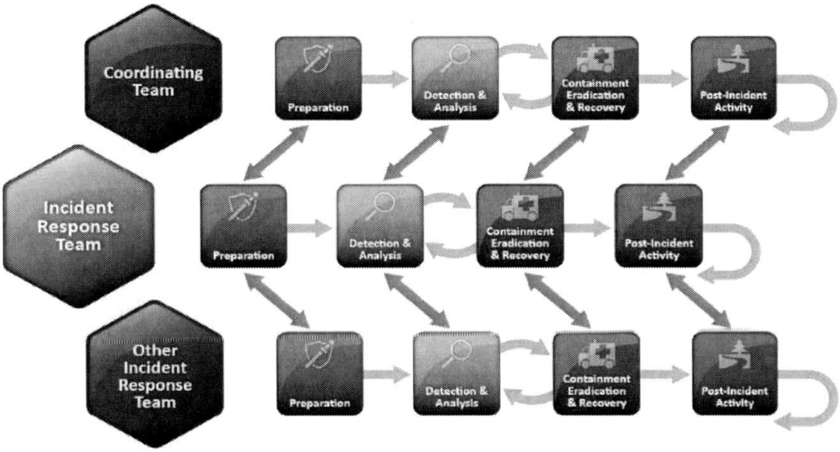

Figure 4-1. Incident Response Coordination.

Table 4-1. Coordination Relationships

Category	Definition	Information Shared
Team-toteam	Team-to-team relationships exist whenever technical incident responders in different organizations collaborate with their peers during any phase of the incident handling life cycle. The organizations participating in this type of relationship are usually peers without any authority over each other and choose to share information, pool resources, and reuse knowledge to solve problems common to both teams.	The information most frequently shared in team-to team relationships is tactical and technical (e.g., technical indicators of compromise, suggested remediation actions) but may also include other types of information (plans, procedures, lessons learned) if conducted as part of the Preparation phase.
Team-tocoordinating team	Team-to-coordinating team relationships exist between an organizational incident response team and a separate organization that acts as a central point for coordinated incident response and management such as US-CERT or an ISAC. This type of relationship may include some degree of required reporting from the member organizations by the coordinating body, as well as the expectation that the coordinating team will disseminate timely and useful information to participating member organizations.	Teams and coordinating teams frequently share tactical, technical information as well as information regarding threats, vulnerabilities, and risks to the community served by the coordinating team. The coordinating team may also need specific impact information about incidents in order to help make decisions on where to focus its resources and attention.

Table 4-1. (Continued)

Category	Definition	Information Shared
Coordinating team-tocoordinating team	Relationships between multiple coordinating teams such as US-CERT and the ISACs exist to share information relating to cross-cutting incidents which may affect multiple communities. The coordinating teams act on behalf of their respective community member organizations to share information on the nature and scope of cross-cutting incidents and reusable mitigation strategies to assist in inter-community response.	The type of information shared by coordinating teams with their counterparts often consists of periodical summaries during "steady state" operations, punctuated by the exchange of tactical, technical details, response plans, and impact or risk assessment information during coordinated incident response activities.

Organizations may find it challenging to build the relationships needed for coordination. Good places to start building a community include the industry sector that the organization belongs to and the geographic region where the organization operates. An organization's incident response team can try to form relationships with other teams (at the team-to-team level) within its own industry sector and region, or join established bodies within the industry sector that already facilitate information sharing. Another consideration for building relationships is that some relationships are mandatory and others voluntary; for example, team-to-coordinating team relationships are often mandatory, while team-to-team relationships are usually voluntary. Organizations pursue voluntary relationships because they fulfill mutual self-interests. Mandatory relationships are usually defined by a regulatory body within the industry or by another entity.

4.1.2. Sharing Agreements and Reporting Requirements

Organizations trying to share information with external organizations should consult with their legal department before initiating any coordination efforts. There may be contracts or other agreements that need to be put into place before discussions occur. An example is a nondisclosure agreement (NDA) to protect the confidentiality of the organization's most sensitive information. Organizations should also consider any existing requirements for reporting, such as sharing incident information with an ISAC or reporting incidents to a higher-level CIRT.

4.2. Information Sharing Techniques

Information sharing is a key element of enabling coordination across organizations. Even the smallest organizations need to be able to share incident information with peers and partners in order to deal with many incidents effectively. Organizations should perform such information sharing throughout the incident response life cycle and not wait until an incident has been fully resolved before sharing details of it with others. Section 4.3 discusses the types of incident information that organizations may or may not want to share with others.

This section focuses on techniques for information sharing. Section 4.2.1 looks at ad hoc methods, while Section 4.2.2 examines partially automated methods. Finally, Section 4.2.3 discusses security considerations related to information sharing.

4.2.1. Ad Hoc

Most incident information sharing has traditionally occurred through ad hoc methods, such as email, instant messaging clients, and phone. Ad hoc information sharing mechanisms normally rely on an individual employee's connections with employees in incident response teams of partner organizations. The employee uses these connections to manually share information with peers and coordinate with them to construct strategies for responding to an incident. Depending on the size of the organization, these ad hoc techniques may be the most cost-effective way of sharing information with partner organizations. However, due to the informal nature of ad hoc information sharing, it is not possible to guarantee that the information sharing processes will always operate. For example, if a particularly well-connected employee resigns from an incident response team, that team may temporarily lose the majority of information sharing channels it relies on to effectively coordinate with outside organizations.

Ad hoc information sharing methods are also largely unstandardized in terms of what information is communicated and how that communication occurs. Because of the lack of standardization, they tend to require manual intervention and to be more resource-intensive to process than the alternative, partially automated methods. Whenever possible an organization should attempt to formalize its information sharing strategies through formal agreements with partner organizations and technical mechanisms that will help to partially automate the sharing of information.

4.2.2. Partially Automated

Organizations should attempt to automate as much of the information sharing process as possible to make cross-organizational coordination efficient and cost effective. In reality, it will not be possible to fully automate the sharing of all incident information, nor will it be desirable due to security and trust considerations. Organizations should attempt to achieve a balance of automated information sharing overlaid with human-centric processes for managing the information flow.

When engineering automated information sharing solutions, organizations should first consider what types of information they will communicate with partners. The organization may want to construct a formal data dictionary enumerating all entities and relationships between entities that they will wish to share. Once the organization understands the types of information they will share, it is necessary to construct formal, machine-processable models to capture this information. Wherever possible, an organization should use existing data exchange standards for representing the information they need to share.[47] The organization should work with its partner organizations when deciding on the data exchange models to ensure that the standards selected are compatible with the partner organization's incident response systems. When selecting existing data exchange models, organizations may prefer to select multiple models that model different aspects of the incident response domain and then leverage these models in a modular fashion, communicating only the information needed at a specific decision point in the life cycle. Appendix E provides a non-exhaustive list of existing standards defining data exchange models that are applicable to the incident response domain.

In addition to selecting the data exchange models for sharing incident information, an organization must also work with its partner organizations to agree on the technical transport mechanisms for enabling the information exchange to occur in an automated fashion. These transport mechanisms include, at a minimum, the transport protocol for exchanging the information, the architectural model for communicating with an information resource, and the applicable ports and domain names for accessing an information resource in a particular organization. For example, a group of partner organizations may decide to exchange incident information using a Representational State Transfer (REST) architecture to exchange IODEF/Real-Time Inter-Network Defense (RID) data over Hypertext Transfer Protocol Secure (HTTPS) on port 4590 of a specific domain name within each organization's DMZ.

4.2.3. Security Considerations

There are several security considerations that incident response teams should consider when planning their information sharing. One is being able to designate who can see which pieces of incident information (e.g., protection of sensitive information). It may also be necessary to perform data sanitization or scrubbing to remove sensitive pieces of data from the incident information without disturbing the information on precursors, indicators, and other technical information. See Section 4.3 for more information on granular information sharing. The incident response team should also ensure that the necessary measures are taken to protect information shared with the team by other organizations.

There are also many legal issues to consider regarding data sharing. See Section 4.1.2 for additional information.

4.3. Granular Information Sharing

Organizations need to balance the benefits of information sharing with the drawbacks of sharing sensitive information, ideally sharing the necessary information and only the necessary information with the appropriate parties. Organizations can think of their incident information as being comprised of two types of information: business impact and technical. Business impact information is often shared in the context of a team-to-coordinating-team relationship as defined in Section 4.1.1, while technical information is often shared within all three types of coordination relationships. This section discusses both types of information and provides recommendations for performing granular information sharing.

4.3.1. Business Impact Information

Business impact information involves how the incident is affecting the organization in terms of mission impact, financial impact, etc. Such information, at least at a summary level, is often reported to higher-level coordinating incident response teams to communicate an estimate of the damage caused by the incident. Coordinating response teams may need this impact information to make decisions regarding the degree of assistance to provide to the reporting organization. A coordinating team may also use this information to make decisions relative to how a specific incident will affect other organizations in the community they represent.

Coordinating teams may require member organizations to report on some degree of business impact information. For example, a coordinating team may require a member organization to report impact information using the categories defined in Section 3.2.6. In this case, for a hypothetical incident an organization would report that it has a functional impact of *medium*, an information impact of *none*, and will require *extended* recoverability time. This high-level information would alert the coordinating team that the member organization requires some level of additional resources to recover from the incident. The coordinating team could then pursue additional communication with the member organization to determine how many resources are required as well as the type of resources based on the technical information provided about the incident.

Business impact information is only useful for reporting to organizations that have some interest in ensuring the mission of the organization experiencing the incident. In many cases, incident response teams should avoid sharing business impact information with outside organizations unless there is a clear value proposition or formal reporting requirements. When sharing information with peer and partner organizations, incident response teams should focus on exchanging technical information as outlined in Section 4.3.2.

4.3.2. Technical Information

There are many different types of technical indicators signifying the occurrence of an incident within an organization. These indicators originate from the variety of technical information associated with incidents, such as the hostnames and IP addresses of attacking hosts, samples of malware, precursors and indicators of similar incidents, and types of vulnerabilities exploited in an incident. Section 3.2.2 provides an overview of how organizations should collect and utilize these indicators to help identify an incident that is in progress. In addition, Section 3.2.3 provides a listing of common sources of incident indicator data.

While organizations gain value from collecting their own internal indicators, they may gain additional value from analyzing indicators received from partner organizations and sharing internal indicators for external analysis and use. If the organization receives external indicator data pertaining to an incident they have not seen, they can use that indicator data to identify the incident as it begins to occur. Similarly, an organization may use external indicator data to detect an ongoing incident that it was not aware of due to the lack of internal resources to capture the specific indicator data. Organizations may also benefit from sharing their internal indicator data with external organizations. For example, if they share technical information pertaining to an incident they are experiencing, a partner organization may respond with a suggested remediation strategy for handling that incident.

Organizations should share as much of this information as possible; however, there may be both security and liability reasons why an organization would not want to reveal the details of an exploited vulnerability. External indicators, such as the general characteristics of attacks and the identity of attacking hosts, are usually safe to share with others. Organizations should consider which types of technical information should or should not be shared with various parties, and then endeavor to share as much of the appropriate information as possible with other organizations.

Technical indicator data is useful when it allows an organization to identify an actual incident. However, not all indicator data received from external sources will pertain to the organization receiving it. In some cases, this external data will generate false positives within the receiving organization's network and may cause resources to be spent on nonexistent problems.

Organizations participating in incident information sharing should have staff skilled in taking technical indicator information from sharing communities and disseminating that information throughout the enterprise, preferably in an automated way. Organizations should also attempt to ensure that they only share an indicator for which they have a relatively high level of confidence that it signifies an actual incident.

4.4. Recommendations

The key recommendations presented in this section for handling incidents are summarized below.

- **Plan incident coordination with external parties before incidents occur.** Examples of external parties include other incident response teams, law enforcement agencies, Internet service providers, and constituents and customers. This planning helps ensure that all parties know their roles and that effective lines of communication are established.

- **Consult with the legal department before initiating any coordination efforts.** There may be contracts or other agreements that need to be put into place before discussions occur.
- **Perform incident information sharing throughout the incident response life cycle.** Information sharing is a key element of enabling coordination across organizations. Organizations should not wait until an incident has been fully resolved before sharing details of it with others.
- **Attempt to automate as much of the information sharing process as possible.** This makes cross-organizational coordination efficient and cost effective. Organizations should attempt to achieve a balance of automated information sharing overlaid with human-centric processes for managing the information flow.
- **Balance the benefits of information sharing with the drawbacks of sharing sensitive information.** Ideally organizations should share the necessary information and only the necessary information with the appropriate parties. Business impact information is often shared in a team-tocoordinating team relationship, while technical information is often shared within all types of coordination relationships. When sharing information with peer and partner organizations, incident response teams should focus on exchanging technical information.
- **Share as much of the appropriate incident information as possible with other organizations.** Organizations should consider which types of technical information should or should not be shared with various parties. For example, external indicators, such as the general characteristics of attacks and the identity of attacking hosts, are usually safe to share with others, but there may be both security and liability reasons why an organization would not want to reveal the details of an exploited vulnerability.

Organizations participating in incident information sharing should have staff skilled in taking technical indicator information from sharing communities and disseminating that information throughout the enterprise, preferably in an automated way. Organizations should also attempt to ensure that they only share an indicator for which they have a relatively high level of confidence that it signifies an actual incident.

APPENDIX A—INCIDENT HANDLING SCENARIOS

Incident handling scenarios provide an inexpensive and effective way to build incident response skills and identify potential issues with incident response processes. The incident response team or team members are presented with a scenario and a list of related questions. The team then discusses each question and determines the most likely answer. The goal is to determine what the team would really do and to compare that with policies, procedures, and generally recommended practices to identify discrepancies or deficiencies. For example, the answer to one question may indicate that the response would be delayed because the team lacks a piece of software or because another team does not provide off-hours support.

The questions listed below are applicable to almost any scenario. Each question is followed by a reference to the related section(s) of the document. After the questions are scenarios, each of which is followed by additional incident-specific questions. Organizations are strongly encouraged to adapt these questions and scenarios for use in their own incident response exercises.[48]

A.1. Scenario Questions

Preparation:

1. Would the organization consider this activity to be an incident? If so, which of the organization's policies does this activity violate? *(Section 2.1)*
2. What measures are in place to attempt to prevent this type of incident from occurring or to limit its impact? *(Section 3.1.2)*

Detection and Analysis:

1. What precursors of the incident, if any, might the organization detect? Would any precursors cause the organization to take action before the incident occurred? *(Sections 3.2.2, 3.2.3)*
2. What indicators of the incident might the organization detect? Which indicators would cause someone to think that an incident might have occurred? *(Sections 3.2.2, 3.2.3)*
3. What additional tools might be needed to detect this particular incident? *(Section 3.2.3)*

4. How would the incident response team analyze and validate this incident? What personnel would be involved in the analysis and validation process? *(Section 3.2.4)*
5. To which people and groups within the organization would the team report the incident? *(Section 3.2.7)*
6. How would the team prioritize the handling of this incident? *(Section 3.2.6)*

Containment, Eradication, and Recovery:

1. What strategy should the organization take to contain the incident? Why is this strategy preferable to others? *(Section 3.3.1)*
2. What could happen if the incident were not contained? *(Section 3.3.1)*
3. What additional tools might be needed to respond to this particular incident? *(Sections 3.3.1, 3.3.4)*
4. Which personnel would be involved i n the containment, eradication, and/or recovery processes? *(Sections 3.3.1, 3.3.4)*
5. What sources of evidence, if any, should the organization acquire? How would the evidence be acquired? Where would it be stored? How long should it be retained? *(Sections 3.2.5, 3.3.2, 3.4.3)*

Post-Incident Activity:

1. Who would attend the lessons learned meeting regarding this incident? *(Section 3.4.1)*
2. What could be done to prevent similar incidents from occurring in the future? *(Section 3.1.2)*
3. What could be done to improve detection of similar incidents? *(Section 3.1.2)*

General Questions:

1. How many incident response team members would participate in handling this incident? *(Section 2.4.3)*
2. Besides the incident response team, what groups within the organization would be involved in handling this incident? *(Section 2.4.4)*

3. To which external parties would the team report the incident? When would each report occur? How would each report be made? What information would you report or not report, and why? *(Section 2.3.2)*
4. What other communications with external parties may occur? *(Section 2.3.2)*
5. What tools and resources would the team use in handling this incident? *(Section 3.1.1)*
6. What aspects of the handling would have been different if the incident had occurred at a different day and time (on-hours versus off-hours)? *(Section 2.4.2)*
7. What aspects of the handling would have been different if the incident had occurred at a different physical location (onsite versus offsite)? *(Section 2.4.2)*

A.2. Scenarios

Scenario 1: Domain Name System (DNS) Server Denial of Service (DoS)

On a Saturday afternoon, external users start having problems accessing the organization's public websites. Over the next hour, the problem worsens to the point where nearly every access attempt fails. Meanwhile, a member of the organization's networking staff responds to alerts from an Internet border router and determines that the organization's Internet bandwidth is being consumed by an unusually large volume of User Datagram Protocol (UDP) packets to and from both the organization's public DNS servers. Analysis of the traffic shows that the DNS servers are receiving high volumes of requests from a single external IP address. Also, all the DNS requests from that address come from the same source port.

The following are additional questions for this scenario:

1. Whom should the organization contact regarding the external IP address in question?
2. Suppose that after the initial containment measures were put in place, the network administrators detected that nine internal hosts were also attempting the same unusual requests to the DNS server. How would that affect the handling of this incident?
3. Suppose that two of the nine internal hosts disconnected from the network before their system owners were identified. How would the system owners be identified?

Scenario 2: Worm and Distributed Denial of Service (DDoS) Agent Infestation

On a Tuesday morning, a new worm is released; it spreads itself through removable media, and it can copy itself to open Windows shares. When the worm infects a host, it installs a DDoS agent. The organization has already incurred widespread infections before antivirus signatures become available several hours after the worm started to spread.

The following are additional questions for this scenario:

1. How would the incident response team identify all infected hosts?
2. How would the organization attempt to prevent the worm from entering the organization before antivirus signatures were released?
3. How would the organization attempt to prevent the worm from being spread by infected hosts before antivirus signatures were released?
4. Would the organization attempt to patch all vulnerable machines? If so, how would this be done?
5. How would the handling of this incident change if infected hosts that had received the DDoS agent had been configured to attack another organization's website the next morning?
6. How would the handling of this incident change if one or more of the infected hosts contained sensitive personally identifiable information regarding the organization's employees?
7. How would the incident response team keep the organization's users informed about the status of the incident?
8. What additional measures would the team perform for hosts that are not currently connected to the network (e.g., staff members on vacation, offsite employees who connect occasionally)?

Scenario 3: Stolen Documents

On a Monday morning, the organization's legal department receives a call from the Federal Bureau of Investigation (FBI) regarding some suspicious activity involving the organization's systems. Later that day, an FBI agent meets with members of management and the legal department to discuss the activity. The FBI has been investigating activity involving public posting of sensitive government documents, and some of the documents reportedly belong to the organization. The agent asks for the organization's assistance, and management asks for the incident response team's assistance in acquiring the necessary evidence to determine if these documents are legitimate or not and how they might have been leaked.

The following are additional questions for this scenario:

1. From what sources might the incident response team gather evidence?
2. What would the team do to keep the investigation confidential?
3. How would the handling of this incident change if the team identified an internal host responsible for the leaks?
4. How would the handling of this incident change if the team found a rootkit installed on the internal host responsible for the leaks?

Scenario 4: Compromised Database Server

On a Tuesday night, a database administrator performs some off-hours maintenance on several production database servers. The administrator notices some unfamiliar and unusual directory names on one of the servers. After reviewing the directory listings and viewing some of the files, the administrator concludes that the server has been attacked and calls the incident response team for assistance. The team's investigation determines that the attacker successfully gained root access to the server six weeks ago.

The following are additional questions for this scenario:

1. What sources might the team use to determine when the compromise had occurred?
2. How would the handling of this incident change if the team found that the database server had been running a packet sniffer and capturing passwords from the network?
3. How would the handling of this incident change if the team found that the server was running a process that would copy a database containing sensitive customer information (including personally identifiable information) each night and transfer it to an external address?
4. How would the handling of this incident change if the team discovered a root kit on the server?

Scenario 5: Unknown Exfiltration

On a Sunday night, one of the organization's network intrusion detection sensors alerts on anomalous outbound network activity involving large file transfers. The intrusion analyst reviews the alerts; it appears that thousands of .RAR files are being copied from an internal host to an external host, and the external host is located in another country. The analyst contacts the incident response team so that it can investigate the activity further. The team is unable to see what the .RAR files hold because their contents are encrypted. Analysis of the internal host containing the .RAR files shows signs of a bot installation.

The following are additional questions for this scenario:

1. How would the team determine what was most likely inside the .RAR files? Which other teams might assist the incident response team?
2. If the incident response team determined that the initial compromise had been performed through a wireless network card in the internal host, how would the team further investigate this activity?
3. If the incident response team determined that the internal host was being used to stage sensitive files from other hosts within the enterprise, how would the team further investigate this activity?

Scenario 6: Unauthorized Access to Payroll Records

On a Wednesday evening, the organization's physical security team receives a call from a payroll administrator who saw an unknown person leave her office, run down the hallway, and exit the building. The administrator had left her workstation unlocked and unattended for only a few minutes. The payroll program is still logged in and on the main menu, as it was when she left it, but the administrator notices that the mouse appears to have been moved. The incident response team has been asked to acquire evidence related to the incident and to determine what actions were performed.

The following are additional questions for this scenario:

1. How would the team determine what actions had been performed?
2. How would the handling of this incident differ if the payroll administrator had recognized the person leaving her office as a former payroll department employee?
3. How would the handling of this incident differ if the team had reason to believe that the person was a current employee?
4. How would the handling of this incident differ if the physical security team determined that the person had used social engineering techniques to gain physical access to the building?
5. How would the handling of this incident differ if logs from the previous week showed an unusually large number of failed remote login attempts using the payroll administrator's user ID?
6. How would the handling of this incident differ if the incident response team discovered that a keystroke logger was installed on the computer two weeks earlier?

Scenario 7: Disappearing Host

On a Thursday afternoon, a network intrusion detection sensor records vulnerability scanning activity directed at internal hosts that is being generated by an internal IP address. Because the intrusion detection analyst is unaware of any authorized, scheduled vulnerability scanning activity, she reports the activity to the incident response team. When the team begins the analysis, it discovers that the activity has stopped and that there is no longer a host using the IP address.

The following are additional questions for this scenario:

1. What data sources might contain information regarding the identity of the vulnerability scanning host?
2. How would the team identify who had been performing the vulnerability scans?
3. How would the handling of this incident differ if the vulnerability scanning were directed at the organization's most critical hosts?
4. How would the handling of this incident differ if the vulnerability scanning were directed at external hosts?
5. How would the handling of this incident differ if the internal IP address was associated with the organization's wireless guest network?
6. How would the handling of this incident differ if the physical security staff discovered that someone had broken into the facility half an hour before the vulnerability scanning occurred?

Scenario 8: Telecommuting Compromise

On a Saturday night, network intrusion detection software records an inbound connection originating from a watch list IP address. The intrusion detection analyst determines that the connection is being made to the organization's VPN server and contacts the incident response team. The team reviews the intrusion detection, firewall, and VPN server logs and identifies the user ID that was authenticated for the session and the name of the user associated with the user ID.

The following are additional questions for this scenario:

1. What should the team's next step be (e.g., calling the user at home, disabling the user ID, disconnecting the VPN session)? Why should this step be performed first? What step should be performed second?

2. How would the handling of this incident differ if the external IP address belonged to an open proxy?
3. How would the handling of this incident differ if the ID had been used to initiate VPN connections from several external IP addresses without the knowledge of the user?
4. Suppose that the identified user's computer had become compromised by a game containing a Trojan horse that was downloaded by a family member. How would this affect the team's analysis of the incident? How would this affect evidence gathering and handling? What should the team do in terms of eradicating the incident from the user's computer?
5. Suppose that the user installed antivirus software and determined that the Trojan horse had included a keystroke logger. How would this affect the handling of the incident? How would this affect the handling of the incident if the user were a system administrator? How would this affect the handling of the incident if the user were a high-ranking executive in the organization?

Scenario 9: Anonymous Threat

On a Thursday afternoon, the organization's physical security team receives a call from an IT manager, reporting that two of her employees just received anonymous threats against the organization's systems. Based on an investigation, the physical security team believes that the threats should be taken seriously and notifies the appropriate internal teams, including the incident response team, of the threats.

The following are additional questions for this scenario:

1. What should the incident response team do differently, if anything, in response to the notification of the threats?
2. What impact could heightened physical security controls have on the team's responses to incidents?

Scenario 10: Peer-to-Peer File Sharing

The organization prohibits the use of peer-to-peer file sharing services. The organization's network intrusion detection sensors have signatures enabled that can detect the usage of several popular peer-to peer file sharing services. On a Monday evening, an intrusion detection analyst notices that several file sharing alerts have occurred during the past three hours, all involving the same internal IP address.

1. What factors should be used to prioritize the handling of this incident (e.g., the apparent content of the files that are being shared)?
2. What privacy considerations may impact the handling of this incident?
3. How would the handling of this incident differ if the computer performing peer-to-peer file sharing also contains sensitive personally identifiable information?

Scenario 11: Unknown Wireless Access Point

On a Monday morning, the organization's help desk receives calls from three users on the same floor of a building who state that they are having problems with their wireless access. A network administrator who is asked to assist in resolving the problem brings a laptop with wireless access to the users' floor. As he views his wireless networking configuration, he notices that there is a new access point listed as being available. He checks with his teammates and determines that this access point was not deployed by his team, so that it is most likely a rogue access point that was established without permission.

1. What should be the first major step in handling this incident (e.g., physically finding the rogue access point, logically attaching to the access point)?
2. What is the fastest way to locate the access point? What is the most covert way to locate the access point?
3. How would the handling of this incident differ if the access point had been deployed by an external party (e.g., contractor) temporarily working at the organization's office?
4. How would the handling of this incident differ if an intrusion detection analyst reported signs of suspicious activity involving some of the workstations on the same floor of the building?
5. How would the handling of this incident differ if the access point had been removed while the team was still attempting to physically locate it?

Appendix B—Incident-Related Data Elements

Organizations should identify a standard set of incident-related data elements to be collected for each incident. This effort will not only facilitate more effective and consistent incident handling, but also assist the organization in meeting applicable incident reporting requirements. The organization should designate a set of basic elements (e.g., incident reporter's name, phone number, and location) to be collected when the incident is reported and an additional set of elements to be collected by the incident handlers during their response. The two sets of elements would be the basis for the incident reporting database, previously discussed in Section 3.2.5. The lists below provide suggestions of what information to collect for incidents and are not intended to be comprehensive. Each organization should create its own list of elements based on several factors, including its incident response team model and structure and its definition of the term "incident."

B.1. Basic Data Elements

- Contact Information for the Incident Reporter and Handler
    - Name
    - Role
    - Organizational unit (e.g., agency, department, division, team) and affiliation
    - Email address
    - Phone number
    - Location (e.g., mailing address, office room number)
- Incident Details
    - Status change date/timestamps (including time zone): when the incident started, when the incident was discovered/detected, when the incident was reported, when the incident was resolved/ended, etc.
    - Physical location of the incident (e.g., city, state)
    - Current status of the incident (e.g., ongoing attack)
    - Source/cause of the incident (if known), including hostnames and IP addresses – Description of the incident (e.g., how it was detected, what occurred)
    - Description of affected resources (e.g., networks, hosts, applications, data), including systems' hostnames, IP addresses, and function
    - If known, incident category, vectors of attack associated with the incident, and indicators related to the incident (traffic patterns, registry keys, etc.)

- Prioritization factors (functional impact, information impact, recoverability, etc.)
- Mitigating factors (e.g., stolen laptop containing sensitive data was using full disk encryption)
- Response actions performed (e.g., shut off host, disconnected host from network)
- Other organizations contacted (e.g., software vendor)
- General Comments

B.2. Incident Handler Data Elements

- Current Status of the Incident Response
- Summary of the Incident
- Incident Handling Actions
  - Log of actions taken by all handlers
  - Contact information for all involved parties
  - List of evidence gathered
- Incident Handler Comments
- Cause of the Incident (e.g., misconfigured application, unpatched host)
- Cost of the Incident
- Business Impact of the Incident[49]

APPENDIX C—GLOSSARY

Selected terms used in the publication are defined below.

Baselining: Monitoring resources to determine typical utilization patterns so that significant deviations can be detected.

Computer Security Incident: See "incident."

Computer Security Incident Response Team (CSIRT): A capability set up for the purpose of assisting in responding to computer security-related incidents; also called a Computer Incident Response Team (CIRT) or a CIRC (Computer Incident Response Center, Computer Incident Response Capability).

Event: Any observable occurrence in a network or system.

False Positive: An alert that incorrectly indicates that malicious activity is occurring.

Incident: A violation or imminent threat of violation of computer security policies, acceptable use policies, or standard security practices.

Incident Handling: The mitigation of violations of security policies and recommended practices.

Incident Response: See "incident handling."

Indicator: A sign that an incident may have occurred or may be currently occurring.

Intrusion Detection and Prevention System (IDPS): Software that automates the process of monitoring the events occurring in a computer system or network and analyzing them for signs of possible incidents and attempting to stop detected possible incidents.

Malware: A virus, worm, Trojan horse, or other code-based malicious entity that successfully infects a host.

Precursor: A sign that an attacker may be preparing to cause an incident.

Profiling: Measuring the characteristics of expected activity so that changes to it can be more easily identified.

Signature: A recognizable, distinguishing pattern associated with an attack, such as a binary string in a virus or a particular set of keystrokes used to gain unauthorized access to a system.

Social Engineering: An attempt to trick someone into revealing information (e.g., a password) that can be used to attack systems or networks.

Threat: The potential source of an adverse event.

Vulnerability: A weakness in a system, application, or network that is subject to exploitation or misuse.

APPENDIX D—ACRONYMS

Selected acronyms used in the publication are defined below.

CCIPS	Computer Crime and Intellectual Property Section
CERIAS	Center for Education and Research in Information Assurance and Security
CERT® /CC	CERT® Coordination Center
CIO	Chief Information Officer
CIRC	Computer Incident Response Capability
CIRC	Computer Incident Response Center

CIRT	Computer Incident Response Team
CISO	Chief Information Security Officer
CSIRC	Computer Security Incident Response Capability
CSIRT	Computer Security Incident Response Team
DDoS	Distributed Denial of Service
DHS	Department of Homeland Security
DNS	Domain Name System
DoS	Denial of Service
FAQ	Frequently Asked Questions
FBI	Federal Bureau of Investigation
FIPS	Federal Information Processing Standards
FIRST	Forum of Incident Response and Security Teams
FISMA	Federal Information Security Management Act
GAO	General Accountability Office
GFIRST	Government Forum of Incident Response and Security Teams
GRS	General Records Schedule
HTTP	Hyper Text Transfer Protocol
IANA	Internet Assigned Numbers Authority
IDPS	Intrusion Detection and Prevention System
IETF	Internet Engineering Task Force
IP	Internet Protocol
IR	Interagency Report
IRC	Internet Relay Chat
ISAC	Information Sharing and Analysis Center
ISP	Internet Service Provider
IT	Information Technology
ITL	Information Technology Laboratory
MAC	Media Access Control
MOU	Memorandum of Understanding
MSSP	Managed Security Services Provider
NAT	Network Address Translation
NDA	Non-Disclosure Agreement
NIST	National Institute of Standards and Technology
NSRL	National Software Reference Library
NTP	Network Time Protocol
NVD	National Vulnerability Database
OIG	Office of Inspector General
OMB	Office of Management and Budget

OS	Operating System
PII	Personally Identifiable Information
PIN	Personal Identification Number
POC	Point of Contact
REN-ISAC	Research and Education Networking Information Sharing and Analysis Center
RFC	Request for Comment
RID	Real-Time Inter-Network Defense
SIEM	Security Information and Event Management
SLA	Service Level Agreement
SOP	Standard Operating Procedure
SP	Special Publication
TCP	Transmission Control Protocol
TCP/IP	Transmission Control Protocol/Internet Protocol
TERENA	Trans-European Research and Education Networking Association
UDP	User Datagram Protocol
URL	Uniform Resource Locator
US-CERT	United States Computer Emergency Readiness Team
VPN	Virtual Private Network

APPENDIX E—RESOURCES

The lists below provide examples of resources that may be helpful in establishing and maintaining an incident response capability.

Incident Response Organizations

Organization	URL
Anti-Phishing Working Group (APWG)	http://www.antiphishing.org/
Computer Crime and Intellectual Property Section (CCIPS), U.S. Department of Justice	http://www.cybercrime.gov/
CERT® Coordination Center, Carnegie Mellon University (CERT® /CC)	http://www.cert.org/
European Network and Information Security Agency (ENISA)	http://www.enisa.europa.eu/activities/cert

Organization	URL
Forum of Incident Response and Security Teams (FIRST)	http://www.first.org/
Government Forum of Incident Response and Security Teams (GFIRST)	http://www.us-cert.gov/federal/gfirst.html
High Technology Crime Investigation Association (HTCIA)	http://www.htcia.org/
InfraGard	http://www.infragard.net/
Internet Storm Center (ISC)	http://isc.sans.edu/
National Council of ISACs	http://www.isaccouncil.org/
United States Computer Emergency Response Team (US-CERT)	http://www.us-cert.gov/

NIST Publications

Resource Name	URL
NIST SP 800-53 Revision 3, *Recommended Security Controls for Federal Information Systems and Organizations*	http://csrc.nist.gov/publications/PubsSPs.html#800-53
NIST SP 800-83, *Guide to Malware Incident Prevention and Handling*	http://csrc.nist.gov/publications/PubsSPs.html#800-83
NIST SP 800-84, *Guide to Test, Training, and Exercise Programs for IT Plans and Capabilities*	http://csrc.nist.gov/publications/PubsSPs.html#800-84
NIST SP 800-86, *Guide to Integrating Forensic Techniques into Incident Response*	http://csrc.nist.gov/publications/PubsSPs.html#800-86
NIST SP 800-92, *Guide to Computer Security Log Management*	http://csrc.nist.gov/publications/PubsSPs.html#800-92
NIST SP 800-94, *Guide to Intrusion Detection and Prevention Systems (IDPS)*	http://csrc.nist.gov/publications/PubsSPs.html#800-94
NIST SP 800-115, *Technical Guide to Information Security Testing and Assessment*	http://csrc.nist.gov/publications/PubsSPs.html#800-115
NIST SP 800-128, *Guide for Security-Focused Configuration Management of Information Systems*	http://csrc.nist.gov/publications/PubsSPs.html#800-128

Data Exchange Specifications Applicable to Incident Handling

Title	Description	Additional Information
AI	Asset Identification	http://csrc.nist.gov/publications/ PubsNISTIRs.html#NIST-IR-7693
ARF	Asset Results Format	http://csrc.nist.gov/publications/ PubsNISTIRs.html#NIST-IR-7694
CAPEC	Common Attack Pattern Enumeration and Classification	http://capec.mitre.org/
CCE	Common Configuration Enumeration	http://cce.mitre.org/
CEE	Common Event Expression	http://cee.mitre.org/
CPE	Common Platform Enumeration	http://cpe.mitre.org/
CVE	Common Vulnerabilities and Exposures	http://cve.mitre.org/
CVSS	Common Vulnerability Scoring System	http://www.first.org/cvss/cvss-guide
CWE	Common Weakness Enumeration	http://cwe.mitre.org/
CybOX	Cyber Observable eXpression	http://cybox.mitre.org/
MAEC	Malware Attribute Enumeration and Characterization	http://maec.mitre.org/
OCIL	Open Checklist Interactive Language	http://csrc.nist.gov/publications/ PubsNISTIRs.html#NIST-IR-7692
OVAL	Open Vulnerability Assessment Language	http://oval.mitre.org/
RFC 4765	Intrusion Detection Message Exchange Format (IDMEF)	http://www.ietf.org/rfc/rfc4765.txt
RFC 5070	Incident Object Description Exchange Format (IODEF)	http://www.ietf.org/rfc/rfc5070.txt
RFC 5901	Extensions to the IODEF for Reporting Phishing	http://www.ietf.org/rfc/rfc5901.txt
RFC 5941	Sharing Transaction Fraud Data	http://www.ietf.org/rfc/rfc5941.txt
RFC 6545	Real-time Inter-network Defense (RID)	http://www.ietf.org/rfc/rfc6545.txt
RFC 6546	Transport of Real-time Inter-network Defense (RID) Messages over HTTP/TLS	http://www.ietf.org/rfc/rfc6546.txt
SCAP	Security Content Automation Protocol	http://csrc.nist.gov/publications/PubsSP s.html #SP-800-126-Rev.%202
XCCDF	Extensible Configuration Checklist Description Format	http://csrc.nist.gov/publications/ PubsNISTIRs.html#NIST-IR-7275-r4

APPENDIX F—FREQUENTLY ASKED QUESTIONS

Users, system administrators, information security staff members, and others withi n organizations may have questions about incident response. The following are frequently asked questions (FAQ). Organizations are encouraged to customize this FAQ and make it available to their user community.

1. What is an incident?

In general, an incident is a violation of computer security policies, acceptable use policies, or standard computer security practices. Examples of incidents are:

- A n attacker commands a botnet to send high volumes of connection requests to one of an organization's web servers, causing it to crash.
- Users are tricked into opening a "quarterly report" sent via email that is actually malware; running the tool has infected their computers and established connections with an external host.
- A perpetrator obtains unauthorized access to sensitive data and threatens to release the details to the press if the organization does not pay a designated sum of money.
- A user provides illegal copies of software to others through peer-to-peer file sharing services.

2. What is incident handling?

Incident handling is the process of detecting and analyzing incidents and limiting the incident's effect. For example, if an attacker breaks into a system through the Internet, the incident handling process should detect the security breach. Incident handlers will then analyze the data and determine how serious the attack is. The incident will be prioritized, and the incident handlers will take action to ensure that the progress of the incident is halted and that the affected systems return to normal operation as soon as possible.

3. What is incident response?

The terms "incident handling" and "incident response" are synonymous in this document.[50]

4. What is an incident response team?

A n incident response team (also known as a Computer Security Incident Response Team [CSIRT]) is responsible for providing incident response services to part or all of an organization. The team receives information on possible incidents, investigates them, and takes action to ensure that the damage caused by the incidents is minimized.

5. What services does the incident response team provide?

The particular services that incident response teams offer vary widely among organizations. Besides performing incident handling, most teams also assume responsibility for intrusion detection system monitoring and management. A team may also distribute advisories regarding new threats, and educate users and IT staff on their roles in incident prevention and handling.

6. To whom should incidents be reported?

Organizations should establish clear points of contact (POC) for reporting incidents internally. Some organizations will structure their incident response capability so that al l incidents are reported directly to the incident response team, whereas others will use existing support structures, such as the IT help desk, for an initial POC. The organization should recognize that external parties, such as other incident response teams, would report some incidents. Federal agencies are required under the law to report all incidents to the United States Computer Emergency Readiness Team (US-CERT). All organizations are encouraged to report incidents to their appropriate Computer Security Incident Response Teams (CSIRTs). If an organization does not have its own CSIRT to contact, it can report incidents to other organizations, including Information Sharing and Analysis Centers (ISACs).

7. How are incidents reported?

Most organizations have multiple methods for reporting an incident. Different reporting methods may be preferable as a result of variations in the skills of the person reporting the activity, the urgency of the incident, and the sensitivity of the incident. A phone number should be established to report emergencies. An email address may be provided for informal incident reporting, whereas a web-based form may be useful in formal incident reporting. Sensitive information can be provided to the team by using a public key published by the team to encrypt the material.

8. What information should be provided when reporting an incident?

The more precise the information is, the better. For example, if a workstation appears to have been infected by malware, the incident report should include as much of the following data as practical:

- The user's name, user ID, and contact information (e.g., phone number, email address)
- The workstation's location, model number, serial number, hostname, and IP address
- The date and time that the incident occurred
- A step-by-step explanation of what happened, including what was done to the workstation after the infection was discovered. This explanation should be detailed, including the exact wording of messages, such as those displayed by the malware or by antivirus software alerts.

9. How quickly does the incident response team respond to an incident report?

The response time depends on several factors, such as the type of incident, the criticality of the resources and data that are affected, the severity of the incident, existing Service Level Agreements (SLA) for affected resources, the time and day of the week, and other incidents that the team is handling. Generally, the highest priority is handling incidents that are likely to cause the most damage to the organization or to other organizations.

10. When should a person involved with an incident contact law enforcement?

Communications with law enforcement agencies should be initiated by the incident response team members, the chief information officer (CIO), or other designated official—users, system administrators, system owners, and other involved parties should not initiate contact.

11. What should someone do who discovers that a system has been attacked?

The person should immediately stop using the system and contact the incident response team. The person may need to assist in the initial handling of the incident—for instance, physically monitoring the system until incident handlers arrive to protect evidence on the system.

12. What should someone do who is contacted by the media regarding an incident?

A person may answer the media's questions in accordance with the organization's policy regarding incidents and outside parties. If the person is not qualified to represent the organization in terms of discussing the incident, the person should make no comment regarding the incident, other than to refer the caller to the organization's public affairs office. This will allow the public affairs office to provide accurate and consistent information to the media and the public.

APPENDIX G—CRISIS HANDLING STEPS

This is a list of the major steps that should be performed when a technical professional believes that a serious incident has occurred and the organization does not have an incident response capability available. This serves as a basic reference of what to do for someone who is faced with a crisis and does not have time to read through this entire document.

1. Document everything. This effort includes every action that is performed, every piece of evidence, and every conversation with users, system owners, and others regarding the incident.
2. Find a coworker who can provide assistance. Handling the incident will be much easier if two or more people work together. For example, one person can perform actions while the other documents them.
3. Analyze the evidence to confirm that an incident has occurred. Perform additional research as necessary (e.g., Internet search engines, software documentation) to better understand the evidence.

Reach out to other technical professionals within the organization for additional help.

4. Notify the appropriate people within the organization. This should include the chief information officer (CIO), the head of information security, and the local security manager. Use discretion when discussing details of an incident with others; tell only the people who need to know and use communication mechanisms that are reasonably secure. (If the attacker has compromised email services, do not send emails about the incident.)
5. Notify US-CERT and/or other external organizations for assistance in dealing with the incident.
6. Stop the incident if it is still in progress. The most common way to do this is to disconnect affected systems from the network. In some cases, firewall and router configurations may need to be modified to stop network traffic that is part of an incident, such as a denial of service (DoS) attack.
7. Preserve evidence from the incident. Make backups (preferably disk image backups, not file system backups) of affected systems. Make copies of log files that contain evidence related to the incident.
8. Wipe out all effects of the incident. This effort includes malware infections, inappropriate materials (e.g., pirated software), Trojan horse files, and any other changes made to systems by incidents. If a system has been fully compromised, rebuild it from scratch or restore it from a known good backup.
9. Identify and mitigate all vulnerabilities that were exploited. The incident may have occurred by taking advantage of vulnerabilities in operating systems or applications. It is critical to identify such vulnerabilities and eliminate or otherwise mitigate them so that the incident does not recur.
10. Confirm that operations have been restored to normal. Make sure that data, applications, and other services affected by the incident have been returned to normal operations.
11. Create a final report. This report should detail the incident handling process. It also should provide an executive summary of what happened and how a formal incident response capability would have helped to handle the situation, mitigate the risk, and limit the damage more quickly.

APPENDIX H—CHANGE LOG

Revision 2 Draft 1—January 2012

Editorial:

- Tightened writing throughout publication
- Made minor formatting changes throughout publication

Technical Changes:

- Expanded material on information sharing (throughout Section 2)
- Updated incident reporting organization listings (Section 2.3.4.3)
- Updated list of common incident response team services (Section 2.5)
- Revised the incident response life cycle diagrams (throughout Section 3)
- Revamped the list of attack vectors (Section 3.2.1)
- Revamped the factors for incident handling prioritization (Section 3.2.6)
- Changed focus from identifying the attacker to identifying the attacking host (Section 3.3.3)
- Expanded the list of possible incident metrics (Section 3.4.2)
- Updated the incident handling scenarios to reflect current threats (old Appendix B, new Appendix A)
- Made minor updates to incident-related data field suggestions (old Appendix C, new Appendix B)
- Updated all of the tools and resources listings (old Appendix G, new Appendix E)
- Updated the Frequently Asked Questions and the Crisis Handling Steps to reflect changes made elsewhere in the publication (old Appendices H and I, new Appendices F and G)

Deletions:

- Removed duplicate material on forensics, pointed readers to SP 800-86 for the same information (Section 3.3.2)
- Deleted material specific to the old incident categories (Sections 4 through 8)
- Deleted the duplicate list of recommendations (old Appendix A)

- Deleted print resources list (old Appendix F)
- Deleted federal agency incident reporting categories (old Appendix J)

Revision 2 Final—August 2012

Editorial:

- Made mi nor revisions throughout publication

Technical Changes:

- Added information sharing as a team service (Section 2.5)
- Converted Table 3-1 into bulleted lists (Section 3.1.1)
- Added a mention of exercises (Section 3.1.1)
- Revised the attack vectors (formerly incident categories) (Section 3.2.1)
- Added SIEM s, network flows as common sources of precursors and indicators (Section 3.2.3)
- Expanded discussion of eradication and recovery (Section 3.3.4)
- Added a section on coordination and information sharing (Section 4)
- Added a table of data exchange specifications applicable to incident handling (Appendix E)

End Notes

[1] An "imminent threat of violation" refers to a situation in which the organization has a factual basis for believing that a specific incident is about to occur. For example, the antivirus software maintainers may receive a bulletin from the software vendor, warning them of new malware that is rapidly spreading across the Internet.

[2] For the remainder of this document, the terms "incident" and "computer security incident" are interchangeable.

[3] http://www.whitehouse.gov/omb/circulars/a130/a130trans4.html

[4] http://csrc.ni st.gov/drivers/documents/FISM A -final .pdf

[5] http://csrc.ni st.gov/publ i cati ons/PubsFIPS.html

[6] http://www.whitehouse.gov/omb/memoranda/fy2007/m07-16.pdf

[7] For example, an organization may want members of its public affairs office and legal department to participate in all incident discussions with the media.

[8] http://www.us-cert.gov/

[9] http://www.us-cert.gov/federal/reportingRequirements.html

[10] See the National Council of ISACs website at http://www.isaccouncil.org/ for a list of ISACs.

[11] http://www.first.org/

[12] GFIRST is specifically for Federal departments and agencies. (http://www.us-cert.gov/federal/gfirst.html)

[13] http://www.antiphishing.org/

[14] http://www.whitehouse.gov/omb/memoranda/fy2007/m07-16.pdf

[15] http://www.ncsl.org/default.aspx?tabid=13489

[16] Information about the Coordinating team model, as well as extensive information on other team models, is available in a C E RT®/CC document titled *Organizational Models for Computer Security Incident Response Teams (CSIRTs)* (http://www.cert.org/archive/pdf/03hb001.pdf).

[17] See NIST SP 800-94, *Guide to Intrusion Detection and Prevention Systems (IDPS)* for more information on IDPS technologies. It is available at http://csrc.nist.gov/publications/PubsSPs.html#800-94.

[18] Teams should word advisories so that they do not blame any person or organization for security issues. Teams should meet with legal advisors to discuss the possible need for a disclaimer in advisories, stating that the team and organization has no liability in regard to the accuracy of the advisory. This is most pertinent when advisories may be sent to contractors, vendors, and other nonemployees who are users of the organization's computing resources.

[19] http://nvd.nist.gov/

[20] FIPS 140-2, *Security Requirements for Cryptographic Modules*, http://csrc.nist.gov/publications/PubsFIPS.html.

[21] A digital forensic workstation is specially designed to assist incident handlers in acquiring and analyzing data. These workstations typically contain a set of removable hard drives that can be used for evidence storage.

[22] The National Software Reference Library (N SRL) Project maintains records of hashes of various files, including operating system, application, and graphic image files. The hashes can be downloaded from http://www.nsrl.nist.gov/.

[23] *Guide to Test, Training, and Exercise Programs for IT Plans and Capabilities,* http://csrc.nist.gov/publicati ons/PubsSPs.html #800-84

[24] http://csrc.nist.gov/publications/PubsSPs.html provides links to the NIST Special Publications on computer security, which include documents on operating system and application security baselines.

[25] Guidelines on risk assessment are available in NIST SP 800-30, *Guide for Conducting Risk Assessments*, at http://csrc.ni st.gov/publ i cati ons/P ubsS Ps. html #800-30-Rev 1.

[26] Information on identifying critical resources is discussed in FIPS 199, *Standards for Security Categorization of Federal Information and Information Systems*, at http://csrc.nist.gov/publications/PubsFIPS.html.

[27] For more information on continuous monitoring, see NIST SP 800-137, *Information Security Continuous Monitoring for Federal Information Systems and Organizations* (http://csrc.nist.gov/publ i cati ons/PubsSPs.html #800-137).

[28] M ore information on SCAP is available from NIST SP 800-117 Revision 1, *Guide to Adopting and Using the Security Content Automation Protocol (SCAP) Version 1.2* (http://csrc.nist.gov/publications/PubsSPs.html#800-117).

[29] NIST hosts a security checklists repository at http://checklists.nist.gov/.

[30] M ore information on malware prevention is available from NIST SP 800-83, *Guide to Malware Incident Prevention and Handling* (http://csrc.nist. gov/publ ications/PubsSPs. html #800-83).

[31] See NIST SP 800-94, *Guide to Intrusion Detection and Prevention Systems,* for additional information on IDPS products. It is available at http://csrc.nist.gov/publications /PubsSPs.html#800-94.

[32] http://nvd.nist.gov/

[33] http://www.us-cert.gov/cas/signup.html

[34] http://csrc.ni st.gov/publications/PubsSPs.html #800-92

[35] M ore information on NTP is available at http://www.ntp.org/.

[36] Incident handlers should log only the facts regarding the incident, not personal opinions or conclusions. Subjective material should be presented in incident reports, not recorded as evidence.

[37] If a logbook is used, it is preferable that the logbook is bound and that the incident handlers number the pages, write in ink, and leave the logbook intact (i.e., do not rip out any pages).

[38] Consider the admissibility of evidence collected with a device before using it. For example, any devices that are potential sources of evidence should not themselves be used to record other evidence.

[39] NIST SP 800-86, *Guide to Integrating Forensic Techniques Into Incident Response,* provides detailed information on establishing a forensic capability, including the development of policies and procedures.

[40] Appendix B contains a suggested list of data elements to collect when incidents are reported. Also, the CERT®/CC document *State of the Practice of Computer Security Incident Response Teams (CSIRTs)* provides several sample incident reporting forms. The document is available at http://www.cert.org/archive/pdf/03tr001.pdf.

[41] The Trans-European Research and Education Networking Association (TE RE NA) has developed RFC 3067, *TERENA's Incident Object Description and Exchange Format Requirements* (http://www.ietf.org/rfc/rfc3067.txt). The document provides recommendations for what information should be collected for each incident. The IETF Extended Incident Handling (inch) Working Group (http://www.cert.org/ietf/inch/i nch.html) created an RFC that expands on TERENA's work—RFC 5070, *Incident Object Description Exchange Format* (http://www.ietf.org/rfc/rfc5070.txt).

[42] NIST SP 800-86, *Guide to Integrating Forensic Techniques into Incident Response,* provides detailed information on establishing a forensic capability. It focuses on forensic techniques for PCs, but much of the material is applicable to other systems. The document can be found at http://csrc.nist.gov/publications/PubsSPs.html#800-86.

[43] Evidence gathering and handling is not typically performed for every incident that occurs—for example, most malware incidents do not merit evidence acquisition. In many organizations, digital forensics is not needed for most incidents.

[44] *Searching and Seizing Computers and Obtaining Electronic Evidence in Criminal Investigations*, from the Computer Crime and Intellectual Property Section (CCIPS) of the Department of Justice, provides legal guidance on evidence gathering. The document is available at http://www.cybercrime.gov/ssmanual/index.html.

[45] General Records Schedule (GRS) 24, *Information Technology Operations and Management Records*, specifies that "computer security incident handling, reporting and follow-up records" should be destroyed "3 years after all necessary follow-up actions have been completed." GRS 24 is available from the National Archives and Records Administration at http://www.archives.gov/records-mgmt/grs/grs24.html.

[46] Metrics such as the number of incidents handled are generally not of value in a comparison of multiple organizations because each organization is likely to have defined key terms differently. For example, most organizations define "incident" in terms of their own policies

and practices, and what one organization considers a single incident may be considered multiple incidents by others. More specific metrics, such as the number of port scans, are also of little value in organizational comparisons. For example, it is highly unlikely that different security systems, such as network intrusion detection sensors, would all use the same criteria in labeling activity as a port scan.

[47] According to the National Technology Transfer and Advancement Act (NTTAA), "all Federal agencies and departments shall use technical standards that are developed or adopted by voluntary consensus standards bodies". See http://standards.gov/nttaa.cfm for more details.

[48] For additional information on exercises, see NIST SP 800-84, *Guide to Test, Training, and Exercise Programs for IT Plans and Capabilities*, which is available at http://csrc.nist.gov/publ ications/PubsSPs.html #800-84.

[49] The business impact of the incident could either be a description of the incident's effect (e.g., accounting department unable to perform tasks for two days) or an impact category based on the cost (e.g., a "major" incident has a cost of over $100,000).

[50] Definitions of "incident handling" and "incident response" vary widely. For example, CERT®/CC uses "incident handling" to refer to the overall process of incident detection, reporting, analysis, and response, whereas "incident response" refers specifically to incident containment, recovery, and notification of others. See http://www.cert.org/csirts/csirt faq.html for more information.

INDEX

A

B

C

D

E

P

R

S

X

Y